CULTURE SMART!

DENMARK

Mark Salmon

·K·U·P·E·R·A·R·D·

ISBN 978 1 85733 884 3

British Library Cataloguing in Publication Data
A CIP catalogue entry for this book is available from the
British Library

First published in Great Britain
by Kuperard, an imprint of Bravo Ltd
59 Hutton Grove, London N12 8DS
Tel: +44 (0) 20 8446 2440   Fax: +44 (0) 20 8446 2441
www.culturesmart.co.uk
Inquiries: sales@kuperard.co.uk

Series Editor Geoffrey Chesler
Design Bobby Birchall

Printed in Turkey

About the Author

MARK SALMON grew up in Ireland, where he practiced law for ten years; he also has an M.A. in English Literature from the National University of Ireland. He emigrated to Denmark in 1999 and, after teaching English and English Law there for fifteen years, he joined a large international shipping company in Copenhagen as Legal Counsel, a position that he still holds. He has traveled extensively in Denmark, Europe, America, and Africa.

The Culture Smart! series is continuing to expand. All Culture Smart! guides are available as e-books, and many as audio books. For the latest titles visit

www.culturesmart.co.uk

The publishers would like to thank **CultureSmart!**Consulting for its help in researching and developing the concept for this series.

CultureSmart!Consulting creates tailor-made seminars and consultancy programs to meet a wide range of corporate, public-sector, and individual needs. Whether delivering courses on multicultural team building in the USA, preparing Chinese engineers for a posting in Europe, training call-center staff in India, or raising the awareness of police forces to the needs of diverse ethnic communities, it provides essential, practical, and powerful skills worldwide to an increasingly international workforce.

For details, visit www.culturesmartconsulting.com

CultureSmart!Consulting and **CultureSmart!** guides have both contributed to and featured regularly in the weekly travel program "Fast Track" on BBC World TV.

contents

contents

Map of Denmark

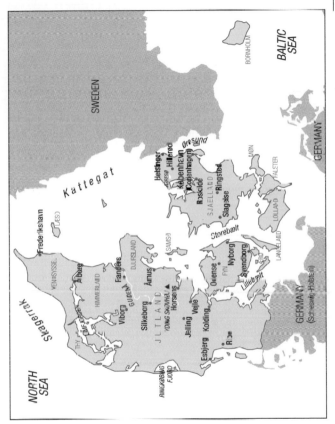

introduction

introduction

Mention Denmark to most people, and they will
think of Viking raiders with horned helmets,
looting and pillaging their way across Europe.
Others may think of one of Denmark's more
famous exports—Carlsberg beer, or the fairy tales
of Hans Christian Andersen. But of the Danes
themselves they will probably know very little.
While there seems to be a cultural stereotype
of the Swedes—oversexed, liberal, and speaking
with a funny accent—there isn't one of the Danes.
As a result our image of Denmark and the Danes
seems to be based largely on what we know of
the Swedes. The Danes seem to have become
lost in a general Scandinavian cultural snapshot,
rather like a little boy at the back of the crowd
in a wedding photograph.

One of the purposes of this book is to set
the record straight   to help show the visitor
to Denmark that there indeed is a difference
between the Danes and their better-known
Scandinavian cousins on the other side of the
Øresund. This is a book for people about people.
It aspires to give you an insight into who the
Danes really are, and what makes them tick. It
will inform you about their history and
geography, and of the roles these have played in
forming the Danish national character. It will

reveal what is behind the way that Danes behave in their daily lives. You will be introduced to the Danish idea of Jante, and its significance in modern Danish society.

You will gain an insider's perspective on Danish family life and the Danish home. You will also see how a little knowledge of Danish attitudes and values can help in meeting and doing business with the Danes. Not only will you learn something of the way in which Danish business works, but there are also many practical tips on how to conduct yourself and what to expect in different situations.

This talented, industrious people have made important contributions to European and world culture. They have created a social model that has been the envy of some and is an example to many, and are justifiably proud of their achievements. It is hoped that, armed with this guide, you will be able to avoid some of the social and cultural pitfalls that foreign visitors are bound to encounter, and that you will get to know and appreciate the Danish people more deeply. While the Danes may be difficult to get to know, they are a friendly, fair-minded, and civilized people who are most certainly worth knowing.

Key Facts

Official Name	The Kingdom of Denmark	Danish: *Kongeriget Danmark*
Capital City	København (Copenhagen)	
Main Cities	Copenhagen, Odense, Århus, Ålborg, Esbjerg	
Area	16,639 sq. miles (43,094 sq. km)	54.02% arable land, 0.19% permanent crops, 45.79% other
Climate	Temperate; humid and overcast; mild, windy winters and cool summers	
Currency	Danish krone (pl. kroner). In 2018, DKk 6.62 = 1 USD DKk 8.59 = 1 GBP	Though Denmark refused to join the Eurozone, the Danish krone remains pegged to the Euro.
Population	5.79 million	Average life expectancy is 81.2 years.
Ethnic Makeup	Scandinavian (86.7%)	Inuit, Faroese, German, Turkish, Iranian, Somali
Family Makeup	The average number of children per family is 1.73.	
Language	Danish. English has been taught in schools for the past 50 years.	German and French are taught as third languages.
Religion:	The State Church is the Danish Folkekirke, or People's Church.	Evangelical Lutheran 76%, Muslim 4%, other 20%

Government	Constitutional monarchy, parliamentary democracy. The monarch has no political power. There is a unicameral People's Assembly or Folketinget (179 seats, incl. 2 from Greenland and 2 from the Faroe Islands). Members elected by proportional representation to serve four-year terms.	
Media	The Danish national broadcasting service, Danmarks Radio, has six public service TV channels and one radio. There are numerous commercial and cable channels.	The largest national newspapers are *Ekstra Bladet, BT, Berlinske Tiden, Jylland Post, MX Metroxpress,* and *Information.*
Media: English Language	Many English-language programs are shown on TV with subtitles.	DR Radio gives an English-language news bulletin at 8:00 a.m. every day. The *Copenhagen Post* is an English-language newspaper.
Electricity	220 volts, 50 Hz	Two-pronged plug used. US visitors will need an adaptor.
Video/TV	PAL System	This is incompatible with US systems.
Internet Domain	.dk	
Telephone	The international access code for Denmark is 45.	There are no local codes for land or cell phones.
Time Zone	Central European Time (GMT/UTC + 1 hour)	Daylight saving from March to October

chapter one

LAND &
PEOPLE

GEOGRAPHICAL SNAPSHOT

Surrounded by sea, except for its slim southern
border with Germany, Denmark is almost an
island. Lying approximately 56° North and 11° East,
it forms a bridge between Scandinavia to the north
and the rest of the European continent to the south,
a position that has resulted in the unique blending
of continental European and Scandinavian values
and ideals that is peculiarly Danish.

In area, Denmark is 16,631 square miles
(43,075 sq. km)—approximately twice the size of
Massachusetts. The peninsula of Jutland makes
up roughly two-thirds of the total landmass, the
rest consisting of around five hundred islands
of varying sizes. The largest of these islands is
Zealand (*Sjælland* in Danish), on which Denmark's
capital, Copenhagen, is situated. The second-
largest island lying between Zealand and Jutland
is the island of Funen (*Fyn*), on which Denmark's
third-largest city, Odense, is located. Zealand and
Funen are separated by a body of water known as
the Storebælt, or Great Belt. This waterway was
spanned by the Storebælt Bridge in 1997, then one

of the largest of its type outside Asia, and briefly the world's largest suspension bridge.

The island of Funen itself is separated from Jutland by the Lillebælt, or "Little Belt," which was first bridged in the 1930s, although the modern bridge was built in the period 1965–70. The rocky island of Bornholm, which lies to the east between Denmark and Sweden, is a popular summer vacation destination for many Danish families. The Danish kingdom also includes two North Atlantic self-governing regions: the Faroe Islands and Greenland.

Denmark's terrain could best be described as flat with some gently rolling plains, the highest point being Ejer Bavnehøj, at some 568 feet (173 meters). The soil is moraine—glacial deposits—from the

Scandinavian and Baltic regions. In Northern and Western Jutland the soil is quite sandy, while in Eastern Jutland and the islands it is more fertile. The exception is Bornholm, which is granite, thinly covered by a layer of moraine.

Most people live near the coast, and there is a strong marine tradition. There are many rivers, the largest of which is the Gudenå, part of the Silkeborg Lake District in Jutland, which is some 98 miles (158 km) long, and is popular with Danes for leisure activities such as boating, fishing, and kayaking. The largest lake in Denmark is the Arresø, on Zealand. There are plenty of sandy beaches on its 4,545-mile (7,314 km) coastline, with the west coast being particularly favored by German tourists. The influx of tourists, while welcome, caused the Danish government to pass a law preventing foreigners from buying vacation homes in Denmark (which are exempt from property taxes), as they were afraid this would drive up house prices beyond the reach of ordinary Danes.

Much of Denmark's natural environment was heavily exploited in the nineteenth century, and as a result only 2 percent of its natural streams remain unaltered, while most of its woodlands are today planted for timber production, recreation, or conservation purposes. The intense cultivation of the land resulted in the loss of many animal species. This exploitation and loss led to a growing environmental awareness among the Danish people. Today restoration projects are widespread throughout the country as a consequence of a nature management act implemented in 1990. Denmark is a nuclear-free zone and has experimented with alternative forms of energy supply—predominantly wind power. Danish businesses are taxed on the amount of carbon dioxide emissions they make, and the European Environmental Agency is located in Copenhagen. Recycling is popular, with approximately 70 percent of all waste being recycled, and public littering is almost unheard of

The population of Denmark is roughly 5.8 million, of which some 70 percent live in urban areas. Approximately two million Danes live in the major cities of Copenhagen, Århus, Odense, and Ålborg. The vast majority (roughly 86.9 percent)

are ethnic Scandinavian, while the remainder consists mainly of Inuit, German, Turkish, Iranian, and Somali. As a result, the influence of foreign cultures on Denmark has been minimal to non-existent. At the time of writing 81.9 percent of the Danish population are over the age of fourteen and the birth rate stands at 10.6 per thousand. If this demographic trend continues, the Danish social welfare system could come under intense pressure in the future, as there will not be enough people working to support those in retirement.

CLIMATE

AVERAGE RAINFALL AND TEMPERATURES IN COPENHAGEN		
(Metric source: Danish Meteorological Institute)		
Month	**Rainfall**	**Temperature**
Jan.	1.9 in (49 mm)	34°F (1°C)
Feb.	1.5 in (39 mm)	32°F (0°C)
Mar.	1.3 in (32 mm)	35.6°F (2°C)
Apr.	1.5 in (38 mm)	44.6°F (7°C)
May	1.7 in (42 mm)	53.6°F (12°C)
Jun.	1.9 in (47 mm)	60.8°F (16°C)
Jul.	2.8 in (71 mm)	64.4°F (18°C)
Aug.	2.6 in (66 mm)	62.6°F (17°C)
Sep.	2.4 in (62 mm)	57.2°F (14°C)
Oct.	2.3 in (59 mm)	48.2°F (9°C)
Nov.	1.9 in (48 mm)	41°F (5°C)
Dec.	1.9 in (49 mm)	37.4°F (3°C)

The Danish climate is officially described as temperate, which is surprising when one takes its northerly location into consideration. It does, however, benefit from the warming waters of the Gulf Stream. The coldest winter months are January and February, when temperatures are around the freezing point. High humidity and cold winds contribute to making things feel much colder, and drive most people indoors during winter. Rainfall is frequent, particularly in July and August, but is spread reasonably evenly throughout the year.

Denmark enjoys long hours of daylight during the summer. The longest days occur in late June, with up to seventeen hours of daylight. In the winter, however, this can fall to eight hours, and the Danes put a great deal of effort into making their hibernatory existence as comfortable as possible.

A BRIEF HISTORY

Denmark has been inhabited since prehistoric times. Agriculture was established around 3000 BCE, and by the Bronze Age (c. 1700–500 BCE) people were burying their dead in burial mounds with their possessions. Sophisticated bronze artifacts have been found in rock tombs from this period. During the succeeding Iron Age (c. 500 BCE–1 CE) climate change caused migration south from Scandinavia into Germany, and there is also evidence of Celtic immigration to Denmark. There was trade with Rome and later, as agricultural land became depleted, conflict with Roman settlements in Gaul.

The ancestors of today's Danes were among the tribes that arrived in the Germanic mass migrations of the fifth to seventh centuries CE. Known as *Daner* or *Dani*, they arrived from southern Sweden in around 500, and became a great power based on the Jutland peninsula, southern Sweden, and—for a brief period in the eleventh century—eastern England, raiding and trading throughout the rest of Europe.

The Viking Period (c. 750–1035 CE)

Scandinavian raiders, mostly Danes and Norwegians, terrorized the British Isles and the Frankish Empire from 750 to 1035 CE. They were given many names by those they dealt with, being called *Normanni* (Northmen) by the Franks, *Gall*, meaning stranger or foreigner, by the Irish, and *Rus* by the Slavs, from which the name Russia comes, derived from the Finnish *ruotsi*—a name for the Svear (modern day Sweden)—which itself came from the word for rowers or a crew of oarsmen. Only the English referred to them, periodically, as Vikings. While the precise etymology of this word remains uncertain, some claim it means a traveler or explorer. The Old Norse expression "to go a-viking" meant to explore. In Old Norse the word *vik* meant a creek or bay, suggesting that a Viking

was one who kept his ship in a bay. Yet another explanation is that it comes from the word *vikingr*, meaning a pirate or raider.

The first mention of Viking raids is recorded in 793, with the plundering and burning of the monastery of Lindisfarne, off the Northumbrian coast of Britain. There is evidence, however, that a large part of Denmark was already an organized state by around 750. This can be seen in the construction of the *Danevirke*, or "Dane work," at around that date. This was a frontier wall of wood and earth built near Hedeby, close to the modern Danish–German border.

The Vikings came from all parts of Scandinavia, but each group had its own overseas sphere of influence. The Danes came to dominate the northeast of England and spread along the coast of Western Europe. In the late ninth century the area of England they conquered and colonized was known as "the Danelaw." Today there is little evidence in Danish society of the more violent aspects of its delinquent past. The Danes are, however, very proud of their brief Viking heritage, and there is a distinct Viking influence in modern Danish jewelry. They have also retained a love of travel and exploration as well as of the sea. One of the largest shipping companies in the world, Maersk, is Danish-owned, and it is one of the largest employers in the Danish private sector.

The history of Denmark as a country ruled by a central figure could be said to have begun in the mid 900s under the reign of Gorm "the old," the son of an invading Norwegian chieftain, Hardegon; the Danish monarchy, the oldest in Europe, traces its lineage back to him. Gorm's son, Harald "Bluetooth," extended and consolidated his rule to all of Denmark, and began the conversion of Denmark to Christianity. Harald's son, Sweyn Forkbeard, and grandsons, Harald II and Knud II (Canute the Great), extended Denmark's rule to England. Knud II, an ardent Christian, completed the conversion of Denmark to Christianity. He was acclaimed King of England by Danes and Anglo-Saxons alike. Denmark's Viking era, and Viking rule in England, ended with the death of his son, Knud III, in 1042.

The Middle Ages

The Middle Ages in Denmark were characterized by violence and civil war that created power vacuums, which rival lords rushed in to fill. Some of the more notable events of the period include the assassination of Knud IV, "the Holy," in 1086, as a result of his introduction of the first personal tax into Denmark. He had been chased out of Jutland by rebellious farmers, who cornered him in a church in Odense on the island of Funen, and stabbed him to death. The assassination in 1131 of Knud Larvard, Duke of Slesvig, the popular nephew of the then aging King Niels (1104-34), led to civil war resulting in the death of the heir to the throne, Magnus the Strong, King Niels, and five of his bishops. The strife eventually ended with the accession to the throne of Knud Larvard's son, as Valdemar I, in 1157. The coat of arms that remains the emblem of Denmark today, three blue lions on a yellow field with small red hearts, dates from this period.

Valdemar "the Great" united a country tired of bloodshed. It was during his reign that the first history of the Danes was produced, written (in Latin) by Saxo Grammaticus. Shakespeare later used one of the accounts from this history as the basis for his tragedy *Hamlet*. Denmark's progressive tradition could be said to have its beginnings during this time. His son, Valdemar II, enacted Denmark's first written laws, known as the "Jutland Code," in 1241, and his descendants introduced laws outlawing imprisonment without just cause, the first Supreme Court, and replaced the old *hof*, or court, with a new and more powerful National Council known as the *Rigsråd*, comprised solely of nobles and senior clergy.

Valdemar I built a castle in the village of Havn, which led eventually to the foundation of the city of Copenhagen. He and Bishop Absalon built Denmark into a major power in the Baltic, competing with the Hanseatic League, the Counts of Holstein, and the Teutonic Knights for trade territory and influence.

The Union of Kalmar, 1397

Dynastic ties between Denmark and Norway had been formed when Margrethe, daughter of Denmark's Valdemar IV Atterdag, married Norway's Håkon VI in 1363. Their five-year-old son Olav succeeded to the Danish throne on the death of his grandfather in 1375, and to the Norwegian throne after the death of Håkon in 1380. When Olav died in 1387, at the age of seventeen, Margrethe I became the official head of state in both countries.

In 1388 rebellious Swedish nobles sought Margrethe's assistance against their king, the

German-born Albert of Mecklenburg. She sent Danish troops to Sweden in return for the Swedes' acknowledgment of her as their sovereign. Finally, in 1397, she constitutionally formalized the Union of Kalmar between the three kingdoms of Denmark, Sweden, and Norway. Her grandnephew, Erik VII of Pomerania, was crowned King of Scandinavia, although she in fact controlled the state's affairs. Under the terms of the Union she agreed to protect the political influence and privileges of the nobility, and each member state retained a fair degree of self-government. The main purpose behind the Union was to fend off the growing influence of the Hanseatic League over trade in the Baltic. This union was tenuous at best and finally fell apart when the Swedes elected their own king in 1523. Norway, however, remained under Danish rule until the Swedes took it over in 1814.

After Margrethe's death in 1412, Erik VII ascended the Danish throne. He is probably most noteworthy for concentrating his power around the Øresund, the sound between Sweden and Denmark and gateway to the Baltic. To this end he moved his capital to Copenhagen in 1417, taking it back from the Bishopric of Roskilde, to which it had been granted by Margrethe in 1375. He built the castle of Helsingør to the north of the city, where the sound was less than three miles wide, installed cannons there, and reinforced the castle of Helsingborg on the opposite shore. Erik curbed the privileges enjoyed by the Hanseatic League, which had become so powerful that it almost controlled the Danish economy at this time. His introduction of the Sound Toll of a silver coin on all passing ships led to open war between the League and Denmark, which the League ultimately lost. In the sixteenth century Denmark grew rich on the increased traffic through the Øresund, which it was able to tax.

Erik was ousted in 1438 by the state councils of both Denmark and Sweden, following an uprising in Sweden, and Denmark fell under de facto aristocratic rule with the figurehead king of Christoffer III on the throne. During this time the members of the Hanseatic League had their old privileges reconfirmed. Christoffer III was succeeded by Christian I in 1448. Christian I was a spendthrift, and is best remembered for instituting the Knighthood of the Order of the Elephant, and founding the University of Copenhagen in 1479. When he died in 1481 his son, Hans, succeeded him and paid off his father's many debts within ten years. King Hans was also responsible for the foundation of the Royal

THE HANSEATIC LEAGUE

The Hanseatic League, or Hansa, was an
alliance of trading cities that maintained a
trading monopoly over most of Northern
Europe and the Baltic states in the late Middle
Ages. It was officially founded in the city of
Lübeck in 1356, and reached the height of its
power in the late 1300s, when there were over
eighty member cities in the alliance. Hansa
cities were strategically located along the main
trade routes. They were independent from
the local nobility, owing allegiance directly to
their respective sovereigns. The League fell
apart in the late 1600s as a result of infighting
and a combination of the social and political
changes that accompanied the Reformation
and the expansion of the Ottoman Empire.

Danish Navy, a new idea in Europe at that time.
He successfully challenged the monopoly of the
Hanseatic League, opening the straits of Denmark
to all in 1511.

Christian II, who succeeded him in 1513, is best
remembered for the "bloodbath of Stockholm," in
which he had eighty Swedish noblemen massacred
following the imprisonment of the unionist
Archbishop of Uppsala. He planned to reduce
the power of both the aristocrats and the Hansa.
They in turn supported the Swedish independence

movement led by Gustav Vasa, later King Gustav of Sweden. The Danish aristocrats renounced allegiance to Christian II, and offered the throne to Frederik, Duke of Slesvig and Holstein, son of Christian I, the younger brother of Hans. In 1523 Christian II was driven out of Denmark. He tried to seize Norway, but was captured and imprisoned for the rest of his life. He died in 1559.

Reformation

Frederik I (1523–33) invited Lutheran preachers to Denmark in an attempt to weaken the influence of the Danish bishops. Among these was a former monk, Hans Tavsen, who preached in Viborg and later Copenhagen to great effect under the protection of the King. On Frederik's death in 1533 the majority of bishops and aristocrats at first refused to elect his eldest son, Christian, as successor, fearing that he would encourage the spread of Lutheranism. (Christian had personally attended Luther's plea at Worms in 1521 and had become a devout Lutheran. His father had let him rule Northern Slesvig, where he carried out a reformation of the Church in the latter end of the 1520s.) Instead they postponed the election, thereby turning Denmark into a de facto aristocratic republic. The deposed Christian II, however, was the first choice of the burghers and the peasants, and the postponement led to a revolt.

The merchant oligarchy in the Hanseatic city of Lübeck had been recently overthrown and the town's mayor offered to help the Danes rid themselves of their aristocratic Council, which had failed to prevent rival Dutch ships entering the Baltic. A German mercenary army was recruited and, led by Count Christoffer of Oldenburg, entered Denmark. A new civil war had begun. Terrified by the revolt, the Council and even the Catholic bishops did an about-face and supported Frederik I's eldest son, who was crowned Christian III (1534–59). Christian and his general, Johan Rantzau, finally succeeded in putting down the rebellion in 1536. Christian III, the "father of the People," set about consolidating his power and to this end was lenient to the merchants and burghers of Copenhagen in return for their support. He arrested Catholic bishops and confiscated Church property for the crown. The Danish Lutheran Church was established as the sole official Church in Denmark, under direct control of the king. This link between Church and state remains today, and the Danish government still has a Ministry for Church Affairs.

Frederick II (1559–88) built the world's first modern observatory, the Uraniborg, on the island of Hven, for the astronomer Tycho Brahe. His son, Christian IV (1588–1648), ascended the throne in a time of prosperity. He left his mark through the construction of new Renaissance towns such as Christianshavn, now part of Copenhagen, Oslo in Norway, and Glückstadt in Holstein, and buildings such as Frederiksborg Castle in

North Zealand and Rosenborg in Copenhagen.
Unfortunately, he was also responsible for involving
Denmark in the Thirty Years' War, which drained
the country of money and resources, and resulted
in the loss of vast amounts of territory. The Swedes
gained control of the island of Gotland as well as
two provinces in Norway following a treaty in 1645.
Further losses followed in a treaty of 1648, namely
the western half of Pomerania and the bishoprics
of Bremen and Verden.

Absolutism

Under Christian's successor, Frederik III (1648–70),
Denmark again went to war with Sweden, only to
lose over one-third of its territory under the Treaty
of Roskilde in 1658. It lost the island of Bornholm,
which later returned to Denmark after a revolt
against Sweden, as well as the rich province of
Skåne and all its other territories in Sweden.

As well as the substantial loss of territory, the
war left Denmark saddled with enormous debts.
Frederik III tried to solve the problem by calling an
assembly of noblemen, commons (burghers), and
clergy to discuss the tax exemptions that had been
granted to them for their efforts during the war.
The nobles refused to give up their tax exemption,
and this resulted in Copenhagen's being put under
siege at the instigation of the clergy and burghers
as well as the king. The siege was lifted only when
the nobles had relinquished their powers of council.
Frederik III then introduced the Act of Absolutist

Succession, giving him and his heirs absolute power, followed by the *Kongeloven*, an absolutist constitution giving him supreme legislative, judicial, and military authority. Frederik III also standardized and modernized the administration and laws. He established the beginnings of the Danish civil service, with departments for commercial activities, military affairs, and foreign affairs. Relations with Sweden improved after 1720 with no more wars and the marriage of the Swedish King Gustav to a Danish princess.

Reform, Napoleon, and the Golden Age

In the late eighteenth century there was very little industry. The nobility still owned about half the land in the country, and agricultural laborers were tied to their estates. In 1784 Crown Prince Frederik assumed control of the government as regent at the tender age of sixteen. Despite his young age he was a genuine reformer, introducing compulsory universal education for all children under fourteen, as well as redistributing land, liberalizing trade, and abolishing feudal obligations. Frederik became King Frederik VI on the death of his father in 1808.

Denmark's membership in the League of Armed Neutrality (with Sweden and Russia) at the outbreak of the Napoleonic wars resulted in a British naval attack on Copenhagen in 1801, which forced Denmark to leave the League. The Danish fleet still represented a threat and the British, fearing it might fall into Napoleon's hands, demanded that it be handed over to them for safekeeping for the duration of the war. When this demand was rejected, Copenhagen was subjected to the first modern rocket attack by the Royal Navy in 1807. As a result of this, Denmark allied herself with Napoleon, and after his defeat was forced by the terms of the Treaty of Kiel (1814) to cede Norway to Sweden, which had sided with the victors.

Although Denmark was by now bankrupt, the 1830s saw the start of a cultural and intellectual "Golden Age." The writer Hans Christian Andersen

and the philosopher Søren Kierkegaard were both products of this renaissance. Another less internationally known product of the age was the theologian Nikolaj Frederik Severin Grundtvig, who was to have a huge influence on

Danish society and culture that is still felt today. Grundtvig stressed the importance of society, and the fact that no one was an island. He hoped that Denmark would reach a stage where "few have too much but fewer too little." He attacked the rote learning of grammar schools and proposed schools where young people would live with their teachers for periods of months learning by "the living word." As a result many "folk high schools" were built from 1840 on, leaving a legacy that survives today in the Danish educational system.

In the political world change was also in the air. Liberal and national movements gained momentum, and the growing bourgeoisie demanded a share in government. Provincial assemblies were formed that had little actual power but provided a platform for debate, leading to the formation of political parties. In 1846 farmers and liberals joined together to form the United Liberal Party, Bondevennernes Selskab. On July 5, 1849, they successfully pressed the king, Frederik VII, to enact a constitution establishing a two-chambered Parliament, the Folketing, with members elected by popular vote, and the Landsting, elected by landowners. The king was made head of the executive, legislative power was shifted to parliament, and an independent judiciary was established. Citizens received the rights of free speech, assembly, and religion, making Denmark one of Europe's leading democracies.

War, Loss, and Political Reform

The liberal and national principles that had so enthused the Danes were also embraced by the German majorities in Schleswig and Holstein, who now sought independence. A first insurrection was suppressed with the aid of Britain and other Great Powers. However, in 1864 the autonomous province of Schleswig in southern Jutland was invaded and captured by a joint Austrian-Prussian army. This was deeply traumatic for the Danes, for whom it was the last of a long series of defeats, including the loss of many of the richest parts of the kingdom.

The country now turned its gaze inward, focusing on improving the lot of those in the poorer areas. Agricultural reforms were undertaken in Jutland, and a new form of nationalism was fostered, stressing the value of the "small" people and rural decency. A Conservative government was elected, and this party retained power until 1901. The Conservatives extended the railway network to cover the entire nation, and there was a boom in the shipbuilding, brewing, and sugar-refining industries, as well as in grain sales to Great Britain. The pace of reform, however, over time, became static.

The social and political changes ushered in by the new constitution were profound, and deeply threatening to the existing elites. They reacted by amending the constitution in 1866 to give greater power to the large landowners by way of a strengthened Landsting. The old National Liberal Party was gradually absorbed by the Højre (the Right) party, which slowly brought together all of the forces of conservatism and dominated the Landsting with the smaller Konservative (Independent Conservatives) party. The Right upheld the equal status of the Landsting and Folketing as well as the right of the King to appoint his own ministers.

In 1871 a socialist labor movement, consisting of different trades and the Social Democratic Party, was formed. The movement was forcefully opposed by the authorities, which led to a series of confrontations and crises between 1871 and 1880. In 1884 the first Social Democrats were elected to the Folketing where they allied themselves with the Left Reform Party. Some opposition groups joined together in 1870 to form Det Forenede Venstre (The United Left) and went on to win a majority in the Folketing two years later.

The United Left demanded a return to the original constitution as well as other reforms. Despite winning a majority in the Lower House, however, they had little effect on the government, and in the late 1880s centrist members of the party began to make overtures to the Right. In March 1894 they reached an agreement that enabled the Right party to stay in power with the support of the United Left in return for the introduction of some more progressive social measures.

Disenchanted with these overtures, a number of United Left politicians under the leadership of J . C. Christensen formed the Venstrereformparti (Left Reform Party) in 1895. They gained in strength until by 1901 it was obvious that the Right party could no longer remain in government with the dwindling support of the United Left.

In 1901 the King, Christian IX, was forced to bow to the inevitable and the Venstrereformparti formed the new government. The pace of reform picked up again and the right to vote was extended to women. The educational principles of Grundtvig were now applied to the educational system as a whole. The Social Democrats won fourteen of the 114 seats in the Folketing in the 1901 election and would go on to become the dominating force in Danish politics in later years. But strains had begun to show in their relationship with the Venstrereformparti since the end of the 1890s. In 1906 the Venstrereformparti lost its majority in the Folketing due to a split in the party, which led to the creation of Det Radikale Venstre (the Social Liberal Party). In 1910 the Venstrereformparti changed its name to Venstre. The four parties that were to dominate Danish politics had now emerged: Venstre, Konservativ, Det Radikale Venstre, and Social Demokratiet. None has ever held an absolute majority in the Danish parliament and Danish politics has been a story of coalition and compromise ever since.

Denmark was neutral during the First World War, and afterward regained northern Schleswig from the defeated Germans, establishing the present southern border with Germany. Between the wars the Social Democrats came to power and, on the back of the Great Depression, introduced sweeping changes that were to lay the foundations of the Danish welfare state.

The Second World War

Denmark was again neutral during the early days of the Second World War, but despite this was invaded by Nazi Germany on April 9, 1940. Until August 1943 the Danes largely ran their own affairs under German supervision. The so-called "Telegram Crisis" occurred when King Christian X celebrated his birthday in 1942. Hitler sent him a 162-word telegram of congratulations, to which the King tersely replied, "Express my best thanks," which infuriated Hitler. The Prime Minister, Vilhelm Buhl, resigned as a result, and was replaced by the more pliable—from the German point of view—Erik Scavenius. As a sign of goodwill the Germans allowed elections to be held in March 1943, in which the Danish Nazi Party received only 3 percent support.

The resistance movement became more organized, and there were increasing acts of sabotage. German reprisals against these led to the resignation of the Danish government on August 30 of that year. The Germans then took absolute control over Danish affairs, and Danish resistance grew rapidly. One of the great successes of this time was the smuggling of 7,000 Danish Jews to Sweden, which was neutral. By the end of the war Denmark had been relatively undamaged, with the exception of the bombardment of Bornholm by the Soviet Union near the end of the war, and the loss of Iceland, which declared itself a republic in 1944.

Postwar

With its wartime experience fresh in mind, Denmark abandoned its policy of neutrality and in 1949 joined NATO. In 1952, together with Norway, Sweden, Finland, and Iceland, it set up the Nordic Council to coordinate Nordic policy. A founding member of the United Nations, it eventually joined the European Community (now the European Union) after a referendum in 1973. Support for the EU in Denmark has always been qualified. Danes suspect that loss of control to the European burcaucrats in Brussels could also mean the loss of their social welfare system. In 1992 they expressed these concerns by narrowly rejecting the Maastricht Treaty, which sought to strengthen European economic and political union. It was only after Denmark was given certain exemptions in relation to the single currency (euro) and joint defense policy, that it adopted the next treaty, the Amsterdam Treaty, in 1998.

In 1953 there was further constitutional reform. The Landsting was abolished, Greenland ceased to be a colony and became an integral part of Denmark (later to receive home rule in 1979), and the female right of succession to the throne was allowed.

The Social Democrats led the way in the establishment of a welfare state in Denmark in the postwar years. The Danish social welfare state today provides Danes with true cradle-to-grave security at the expense of very high taxes. The present government, led by Venstre, a liberal party, has attempted to ease the tax burden somewhat by preventing a rise in taxation, but the system is now so ingrained in the country that no political party would attempt a major change.

Modern Denmark is a country largely at ease with itself. The status quo is threatened by changing demographics, with the number of retired people growing in proportion to the employed. This may lead to an economic crisis as those claiming social benefits begin to outnumber those paying tax. Harsher world economic conditions also pose a threat as the Danish social welfare system is predicated on a high employment level. Maintaining a high level of employment has been a constant challenge since the economic downswings of the 1970s, precipitated by the oil crisis of 1973–74. Yet another threat to the Danish way of life is the perceived danger of European Federalism and the consequent harmonization of social welfare benefits and taxation in Europe to the detriment of the Danish system. Taken together, all these factors could lead to adjustments to the social welfare model and the possible abandonment of the ideal of benefits for all.

CITIES

Lying on the eastern coast of Zealand, the capital, Copenhagen, has a population of close to 2 million (including the greater Copenhagen area). It is the largest city in Denmark, and one of the largest in Scandinavia. As with most capital cities, its inhabitants consider themselves to be a little superior to the rest of the country, and this feeling has spread to the rest of Zealand. This has given rise to a friendly rivalry between the island and the rest of the country.

Århus (population circa. 273,077) is a university city on the eastern coast of central Jutland and serves as the region's cultural capital. Almost 25,000 of the town's population are students at the university.

Odense, on the island of Funen, is perhaps most famous as the birthplace of Hans Christian Andersen. It is a pretty university city of some 178,210 inhabitants.

Ålborg, in North Jutland, is a small city of some 136,000 citizens. It straddles the Limfjord, which divides North Jutland in two. Its primary claim to fame is as the leading producer of aquavit, a form of Danish schnapps.

While each of the major cities has its own cultural identity, residents of Ålborg, Århus, and Odense would probably feel they have more in common with each other than with those of the capital, although this rivalry would probably go unnoticed by most visitors. Most Danes live in

urban areas of one kind or another, but outside
these urban/rural divides are evident.

WHEN LEFT IS RIGHT: GOVERNMENT AND POLITICS
The Danish Electoral System
Denmark is a constitutional monarchy with
a unicameral parliament, the Folketing. The
Folketing consists of 179 seats, of which two are
from Greenland and two from the Faroe Islands.
Members are elected to the Folketing on the basis
of proportional representation, and serve a four-
year term. The Danish system of proportional
representation is quite complex, and any party
receiving at least 2 percent of the national vote
is entitled to representation. This results in a
multiplicity of parties in the Folketing. Politically

Denmark consists of five administrative regions subdivided into 98 municipalities, or *kommuner.*

Political Parties

There are nine major political parties in Denmark. The two largest are Socialdemokratiet, the Social Democrats, and Dansk Folkeparti, the Danish People's Party. Politics in Denmark is conducted mainly through consensus, and political attitudes are generally moderate. As a result of there being so many parties Denmark has been governed predominantly by coalition or minority governments since the Second World War. Danes are politically active, and voter participation is usually above 85 percent. The parties are listed in descending order according to their percentage share of the vote in 2015.

Socialdemokratiet (the Social Democrats)

The Social Democrats are in favor of a significant redistribution of income. They want to maintain a large state apparatus and collectively finance core state services such as health care, education, and infrastructure.

Dansk Folkeparti (the Danish People's Party)

The Danish People's Party could best be described as conservative, nationalist, and social-democrat. It runs on an anti-immigration platform and is opposed to participation in the European Union. It made its debut in the elections of 1998.

Venstre (the Liberal Party)

Venstre is a free-market, liberal party. It advocates lower taxes and less government interference in corporate and individual life.

Enhedslisten (the Red–Green Alliance)

On the far left of the Danish political spectrum, Enhedslisten is an eco-socialist party governed by collective leadership. Its aims are to create an environmentally friendly socialist democracy in Denmark and internationally. It is traditionally opposed to Danish membership of both the EU and NATO.

Liberal Alliance

Formerly New Alliance, Liberal Alliance are a center right, classical liberal party formed in 2007 by former members of the Social Liberal Party and the Conservative People's Party.

Alternativet (the Alternative)

Broadly speaking, the Alternative are a center-left green party founded in 2013 by former Social Liberal Party members. The party does not offer a traditional manifesto, but rather develops it by means of consultation at so called "political laboratories," where anyone identifying with its values is invited to take part.

Det Radikale Venstre (the Radical Liberal Party, officially the Danish Social Liberal Party)

Radikale Venstre is in the center of the Danish political spectrum. They are a social liberal party in favor of a combination of a free-market economy with a state role. They also seek social reform and can be loosely compared to the Democratic Party in the United States.

Socialistisk Folkeparti (Socialist People's Party)
With an ideology lying somewhere between Communism and social democracy, the Socialist People's Party was founded in 1956, following a split with the Danish Communist Party. It is very wary of Europe and has in the past campaigned vigorously against many European integrationist policies such as the single currency.

Det Konservative Folkeparti (the Conservative People's Party)
The Conservative People's Party is, as its name suggests, a conservative liberal party.

DENMARK AND THE WORLD

The role of Denmark in foreign affairs is based heavily on its membership in three organizations, the United Nations, NATO, and the EU, as well as on the principle of Nordic cooperation. Danish foreign policy emphasizes its role in the area of relations with developing nations, and as a result it is one of the very few nations to exceed the United Nations international aid commitment of contributing 0.7 percent of its Gross National Income in official development assistance.

Denmark is a strong supporter of the principle of international peacekeeping, and Danish forces have been involved in many UN peacekeeping missions, as well as the American-led alliance in Iraq.

A strong supporter of the integration of the countries of central and eastern Europe into the West, Denmark has been active in coordinating Western assistance to the Baltic States and played a crucial role in the entry of some of the former Soviet Bloc countries to the EU during its presidency of that union.

Denmark has been a member of NATO since its foundation in 1949 and former Danish Prime Minister Anders Fogh Rasmussen served as Secretary General of NATO from 2009 to 2014. Relations between Denmark and the USA cooled in the period 1982–88, when Denmark adopted specific positions on nuclear and arms control issues that were at odds with the views of the US government. Since then, however, Denmark has been broadly supportive of US policy objectives within the alliance, and membership in NATO remains popular in Denmark.

The Danes have always been reluctant Europeans, mainly due to their suspicion of large centralized government and their fears that a united Europe could spell the end of their social welfare system as it is today. When they rejected the Maastricht Treaty in 1992, they forced a redrafting that included several exemptions for Denmark in the areas of common defense and single currency, as well as EU citizenship and aspects of legal cooperation. This redrafted treaty, the Amsterdam Treaty, was then approved by the Danish people in a referendum in 1998. In a further plebiscite in 2000 the Danes also decided not to join the euro.

THE DANISH SOCIAL WELFARE MODEL

This is the way in which Denmark organizes and funds its social security, health service, and educational system. Its guiding principle is that all citizens should receive benefits, regardless of whether they are employed or not, as long as they fulfill the conditions. The system is universal, which is to say it covers everyone, while the benefits themselves are given to the individual, for example, a married woman's rights are independent of her husband's.

The state pays the largest portion of the funding for the system, financing it through general taxation rather than through earmarked contributions (as is the case in the UK, for instance). Because of this heavy state involvement, taxes in Denmark are comprehensive and high. Under the system both the health service and education are free to all, while other services, such as child care, are heavily subsidized. As a result, while Denmark is a capitalist market economy, there is less inequality in the distribution of income, and the concentration of wealth and power in the hands of a few is inhibited. This could be said to reflect Grundtvig's ideal of few having too much but fewer too little.

The cost of maintaining the welfare state has been high. During the 1980s and 1990s there was a massive foreign trade deficit, interest rates were in excess of 18 percent, and huge foreign loans had to be taken out to cover the deficit.

The future of Denmark's welfare state is now being hotly debated. In the past it was always politically important to aim at full employment, but this has not been possible since the mid 1970s. It was never intended that so many people would receive benefits for so long a period of time as has been the case in recent years. Added to this are the demographic strains of an aging population coupled with a low birth-rate. As a result the financing of the welfare state has become problematic, and the system has had to accommodate this through changes and cuts while maintaining its broad principles.

Conditions in the Danish labor market are regulated through collective agreements between employers and employees that provide for matters such as maternity leave, sickness benefits, and pensions. There is a growing gap between those who are covered by such agreements and the unemployed, who are not—a situation that is in conflict with the principle of equality in the Danish social welfare model. The solution to this problem is the subject of much debate today.

SOME FAMOUS DANES

Tycho Brahe (1546–1601) The first great observational astronomer, author of *De Nove Stella*

Nikolaj Frederik Severin Grundtvig (1783–1872) Theologian, poet, and visionary educationalist, founder of the People's High Schools for adult education

Hans Christian Andersen (1805–75) Writer. Considered one of the world's greatest storytellers.

Søren Kierkegaard (1813–55) Philosopher and writer on theology. Later embraced by the existentialist philosophical movement.

Carl August Nielsen (1865–1931) Composer and conductor

Georg Jensen (1866–1935) Designer, jeweler, and silversmith

Niels Bohr (1885–1962) Nobel Prize–winning physicist

Karen Blixen (Isak Dinesen)(1885–1962) Writer

Jørn Utzon (1918–2008) Architect

Bille August (1948–) Film director

Lars von Trier (1956–) Film director

Peter Høeg (1957–) Novelist

Kevin Magnussen (1992-) Formula 1 Racing Driver

Caroline Wozniacki (1990 -) Tennis Player

VALUES & ATTITUDES

THE LAID BACK NEIGHBOR TO THE SOUTH

It is, of course, almost impossible to characterize a people without some generalization, which will always have exceptions. With this proviso in mind, the observations that follow are intended to be a starting point, or a set of signposts, for your own discovery of Danish culture and society.

Denmark's long history, and its particular location in relation to the rest of Scandinavia, has contributed to the differences that exist between the Danes and the other Scandinavian nations. While they share many of their neighbors' values and attitudes, there are differences in emphasis. The other nations of the region regard the Danes as being somewhat lax in the upholding of traditional Scandinavian values, leading to their characterization of Denmark as "the loose woman to the south." Danes are generally considered by other Scandinavians to be more genial and easygoing. The visitor will not find them as shy as other Scandinavians. A popular joke in Denmark is "How do you know a Swedish extrovert?" Answer: "When he talks he looks at your shoes instead of his own."

In general the Danes tend to be more relaxed and less formal than other Scandinavians. In the business world, however, they are regarded as tough negotiators with a tendency to do business faster. They are also perceived as being more independent minded than other Scandinavians, and are regarded by many in the region as its best salesmen.

One difference is in their attitude to alcohol. In other Scandinavian countries the sale of alcoholic spirits and strong beers is strictly regulated through government-administered shops, where the prices are so high as to make even the most hardened drinkers' thoughts turn to abstinence. In Denmark, on the other hand, spirits and strong beers are on sale in most supermarkets and stores at prices less likely to induce coronary and financial thrombosis. There are strong traditions of brewing and consumption of beer, with the world-renowned Carlsberg brewery at the forefront. Every year, extra-strong beers are issued for the Christmas and Easter seasons, called "Christmas brew" and "Easter brew." Their arrival is heralded by advertising campaigns in the media, and is eagerly anticipated by the beer-loving Danes. At one point, in order to stem the flow of people across the border to Germany in search of cheap alcohol and cigarettes, the Danish government reduced the excise duties on these items with great success. Such a response would be highly unlikely in Sweden or Norway.

While Danish society operates largely on the basis of consensus, there is a greater tolerance for individuality than in the other Scandinavian lands. The Danes like their rebels, and respect alternative subcultures. They do, however, move swiftly, if possible, to find a way to incorporate these subcultures into the mainstream by giving them an official stamp of approval. The so-called "Freetown" of Christiania in Copenhagen is a case in point.

Christiania

Christiania, located in an abandoned former military barracks in Christianshavn on the outskirts of the city, was founded in 1970 by a group of people dedicated to "alternative" living, based on communal principles and freedom from what they saw as the restrictions of mainstream Danish cultural values. There were several attempts by the authorities to remove these squatters from the area, which is owned by the Ministry of Defense, but these were defeated by a combination of the sheer size of the area and the number of people involved. In 1972, by way of compromise, it was decided to give the area the status of a "social experiment" in return for the residents' undertaking to pay for their use of water and electricity.

Since then relations between the residents of Christiania and successive governments have been strained. A particularly thorny issue has been the availability of soft drugs for sale at various stalls in the part of Christiania known as "Pusher Street." Plans for the normalization of Christiania were drawn up by the Ministry of Defense in 1990 entitled "Aims and Means." Since then the story of Christiania has been one of police raids on Pusher Street and protests from the residents against the normalization plans. In 2004 the government passed a law officially abolishing the collective, but since then has been negotiating back and forth with the residents over plans for future development of the area. In the meantime the area is still subject to regular drug raids by the police.

THE JANTE LAWS (*JANTELOVEN*)

The Jante Law, or *Jantelov*, is a set of principles that stems from a novel written in 1933 by the Norwegian/Danish writer Aksel Sandemose titled *A Fugitive Crosses His Tracks*. Set in the fictitious Jutland town of Jante, it deals with the less attractive side of Scandinavian small-town thinking. It had a tremendous impact on Scandinavia in general, and echoes of the Jante Law can still be heard today in Denmark, though not as much as in other Scandinavian countries.

THE JANTE LAW

Never assume you are somebody important.
Never assume you are as good as we are.
Never assume you are wiser than we are.
Never assume you are better than we are.
Never assume you know more than we do.
Never assume you are more than we are.
Never assume you will amount to anything.
You are not entitled to laugh at us.
Never think that anyone cares about you.
Never think that you can teach us anything.

Danes in general are not a flashy people, preferring modesty and self-restraint. Dress codes that emphasize hierarchy are largely ignored, especially in the workplace. It is, for example,

perfectly acceptable on most occasions to go to the
opera or ballet more casually dressed than is usual
in other countries, with the exception of special
or first nights. Danes tend to judge people not by
what they have but by who they are, and boastful
behavior is not tolerated. One should avoid being
regarded as a *blær*, or show-off, at all costs. This
is not to say that the average Dane will go to the
same lengths as the Swedes in following the Jante
Law. There are plenty of signs of wealth to be seen
on the streets of Copenhagen, such as expensive
cars, jewelry, and clothes. The Danes, however,
regard these things not as ostentatious status
symbols, but rather as the rewards of hard work
and accomplishment, and therefore as perfectly
justifiable.

While the Jante Law warns against the dangers
of individualism, the Danes are arguably the most
individualistic Scandinavians, and Denmark is the
Scandinavian country where the entrepreneurial
spirit thrives best. Among young Danes the Jante
Law is seen as somewhat old-fashioned and
something to be either criticized or laughed at.
Many of its tenets, however, are still practiced in
Denmark today, in the guise of equality and social
cohesion. It is perhaps ironic that Sandemose, the
creator of the Jante Law, wrote his book as a form of
criticism of the type of society that these principles
produce. This is a point that seems to have gone
largely unnoticed in Danish society as a whole.

PRIDE AND PREJUDICE—DANISH NATIONALISM

Modern Danish nationalism is not aggressive. Though few Danes will let the opportunity for some loyal flag waving go by, they have neither the imperial past of Great Britain nor the cultural, political, and financial dominance of America to fuel it. Danes are quietly and confidently proud of their country and its achievements. That said, the visitor to Denmark may at times feel that the Danes are, to an extent, smug, if not arrogant, when comparing their country to others. They feel that they have achieved a near perfect society, or at least one that is closer to perfection than most others. They will very readily criticize other countries for their lack of care for the less fortunate, for being class-ridden, or for corruption in high places.

Like most nations the Danes define themselves in opposition to their neighbors. Not as stiff and formal as the Swedes, but as level-headed and classless, and as efficient as, but more imaginative than, the Germans. The Danes see themselves as a nation of hardworking, reliable, diligent, relaxed, and informal people. The visitor to Denmark will see plenty of evidence of Danish nationalism in the Danish flags waving outside every church, on buses during public holidays, and clutched in the hands of friends and relatives welcoming home their loved ones at the airport. Unlike many other people, Danes will fly the flag at important family occasions such as birthdays, anniversaries, and weddings.

Denmark gives a lot to overseas development, roughly 0.85 percent of GNP since 1992. This reflects the Danes' perception of themselves as a generous nation, particularly when it comes to underdeveloped countries. They like to think of themselves as a voice for peaceful coexistence in the world community and as a country that is open to the less fortunate. In recent times, however, this perception has taken a knock as a result of, among other things, Denmark's participation in the conflict in Iraq, as well as the rise of a new kind of nationalist attitude toward the issue of immigration and the ever-increasing popularity of the Danish People's Party in national elections.

THE DANNERBROG

There is a lovely legend about the Danish flag, or Dannebrog, meaning "red cloth," that states that it fell from heaven during a battle in Estonia on June 15, 1219. It was picked up by the Danish Bishop Anders, and the Estonians, seeing this as a sign from God and realizing that the fight was lost, surrendered and promptly converted to Christianity.

In reality the flag was the banner of the German order of knights known as the Knights of Saint John, later the Knights of Malta, which tore itself loose during the battle and landed among its Danish contingent. To celebrate the victory King Valdemar adopted the flag as the symbol of the Danish army and it was later adopted as the national flag of Denmark. The event is still celebrated today and on June 15, Valdemar's Day, the flag is flown across the country. The Dannebrog also shares the distinction with the British Union Jack, the Stars and Stripes, and the Tricolore, of being one of the few national flags to have its own name.

Europe's Oldest Monarchy

The Danish royal family can trace its lineage in an unbroken line back to Gorm the Old in 950 CE, thus making it the oldest monarchy in Europe.

The Danes are very proud of their monarch, who remains a popular figure among young and old alike. The present Queen, Margrethe II, succeeded to the throne in 1972 and is Denmark's first female monarch since 1412. The monarchy itself, and Queen Margrethe in particular, have done much to minimize the sense of privilege that usually separates the royal family from the general public. The Queen is more extroverted and gregarious than her British cousin, and has been involved in spheres of Danish life outside the duties one would normally expect of a monarch. She is an accomplished artist, and has illustrated stamps, playing cards, and an edition of *Lord of the Rings*. She has also translated Simone de Beauvoir's *All Men Are Mortal* from French into Danish. The monarchy has had its share of scandals, and while these have been reported in the media they have not been dwelled on.

In general the Danish royal family are close to their people and not afraid of showing their feelings in public. Many people have commented, upon meeting them, on how "normal" they seem. The Danish court, however, runs on a strict set of rules and protocols just like any other in Europe, with all the pomp and ceremony one would expect from royalty, if on a less grand scale than that of Britain. This unique mixture of personal style with old traditions seems to have ensured the future of the Royal House of Denmark. As a result most Danes see no conflict whatsoever between the principles of equality that they hold so dear and the monarchy, with all its implications of class and privilege.

IMMIGRATION
Immigration has long been a fact of life in Denmark, and immigrants have become an integral

part of Danish society. The majority are from Middle Eastern and African backgrounds. Many sons and daughters of immigrants occupy positions of respect and influence in the media and politics. With the influx of immigrants came changes to the Danish cultural landscape. The newcomers brought with them their native cuisines, and many opened specialist shops to supply the vegetables, herbs, and spices used in their national dishes, which have gained in popularity with native Danes. Small "Mom and Pop" stores or kiosks, owned and run by immigrant families, sprang up around the country. Today, if you visit a dentist or doctor in Denmark, he or she could well be a second-generation immigrant. Because of its high taxes, however, Denmark remains generally unattractive to highly skilled immigrant workers.

Low-skilled immigrant workers have found it difficult to gain a foothold in the Danish labor market owing to problems with the language requirements, and many have found that they are better off living on the generous state welfare benefits. Some Danish employers have, however, tried to accommodate cultural differences, such as by setting up prayer rooms for their Muslim employees.

The influx of immigrants to Denmark has stimulated much debate in the country, in particular as to how they can be integrated into Danish society. If you speak on the subject to Danes you will soon discover that when they talk about the "immigration problem" they are usually referring to immigrants

from a Middle Eastern, Muslim background. Opinions on the question are varied, and split mainly along lines of age, with a majority of older Danes in favor of tougher immigration policies while the young are generally more liberal. It perhaps does not help the visitor's perception of the issue in Denmark that the Danish word for immigrant is *indvandre*, which to English-speakers looks misleadingly like "invader." (The actual Danish word for invader is *angriber*.) In recent times the immigration question has become something of a "hot potato" in Danish politics. The 2015 election saw support for the Danish People's Party (Dansk Folkeparti) rise to 21 percent of the national vote, making them the second largest party in the country.

While there is a popular perception that immigrants are responsible for a lot of crime in Denmark, statistics show that 83 percent of crime in Denmark is committed by individuals of Danish origin and 14 percent by individuals of non-Western descent.

There are also social and religious issues involved—the conservative traditions of Islam in relation to women, for example, are in direct opposition to Danish values of equality. Denmark recently moved to ban the wearing of full face veils, the traditional dress of more orthodox Muslim women. The question of integration still remains open, but the current trends in Denmark are toward a more restrictive approach than in the past. Visitors should tread carefully on the topic of immigration, which is best avoided if at all possible. It can lead to heated debate, and many Danes are very sensitive about the issue as it raises conflicts not only with the image they have of themselves but also with the values that are a part of their culture.

"TOEING THE LINE"

The Danes are a very orderly people. They like things to be organized. In many shops a ticket system is used to keep people in line. On entering the shop you simply take a numbered ticket and then wait until your number is called, at which time you will receive assistance. Try to bypass this system at your own peril.

The Danish penchant for organization can also be seen in the number of associations, or *forening*, that exist in the country. No matter what your hobby, sport, or interest, you are sure to find an association for it in Denmark. Once you join the association you will in all likelihood receive the association's magazine on a monthly basis. All of these associations can apply to the state for funding and, if granted, will receive it according to the number of members they have. They are therefore understandably anxious to hold on to their members. As a result one can sometimes still be receiving the monthly newsletter of an association one left over a year ago.

Organization starts at a very early age in Denmark. Children go to state-subsidized day-care centers, where their daily routine is planned and organized by state-approved professionals known as *pædagoger*. Because the vast majority of children in Denmark go through this system from a very early age, the values and attitudes that they imbibe tend to be somewhat uniform. It is therefore not surprising that there is so much consensus in Denmark.

Great emphasis is put on the need for children to discuss their problems with each other and with their elders so that a compromise can be reached. As a visitor to the country you will find, therefore, that Danes love discussing things, and Danish television is full of discussion and debate programs on every subject from God to politics.

ROMANTICISM AND OPTIMISM
"Romance" and "romantic" are not words one immediately associates with Scandinavians. Danes are, however, romantic souls, if a little reticent about displaying this side of their character. Their

outlook on life is, generally, a romantic one. Like other Scandinavians, the Danes love nature, and will enthuse endlessly about the landscape of either their own country or one they have visited. In Denmark this attitude, combined with good old-fashioned Danish practicality, has led to some very progressive environmental policies from the government with the full support of the population.

Danes have a tendency to try to see the positive side of any situation. When it comes to their own country they may acknowledge that there are problems but they believe that generally things are pretty all right, especially in comparison with the rest of the world. Danes are great travelers, and many young people take time off between high school and college to travel around the world. When you talk to them they will, in general, be enthusiastic about the countries that they have visited and give you a positive picture of them.

MARRIAGE AND SEXUALITY

The institution of marriage is on the wane in Denmark, where 60 percent of first-born children are born out of wedlock. In 1989 Denmark became the first country to legalize same-sex marriage, and today such partnerships are, at least in the bigger cities, accepted without a raised eyebrow. Another law followed in 2000, giving same-sex couples the right to custody of children from a previous heterosexual marriage. As well as this, because of the excellent

public child-care system, the link between marriage
and parenthood that is almost sacrosanct in many
other countries simply does not exist in Denmark,
nor is it necessary from a practical point of view. A
large number of Danish people cohabit and raise
their children without the need for official sanction
from Church or state. Denmark also has a divorce
rate of 50 percent, so single-parent families are
common. When the Danish Prince Joachim and his
Hong Kong–born wife Alexandra divorced there
was plenty of media coverage in Denmark, but there
was none of the controversy that surrounded, for
example, the royal divorces that took place in the
United Kingdom. Most Danes saw it simply as a
reflection of modern society.

The Danish state Church, the Folkekirke, has
also acknowledged the present state of matrimony
in Denmark. In a report on same-sex marriage
in Denmark, written in 1997, the commission of
Bishops wrote that, "As a consequence of changes

in family patterns, marriage is not any longer dominating as a frame around common life." A point that the visitor should take into account is that Danes, as a result, have a tendency to refer to the partner they live with, when speaking English, as their "husband" or "wife," whether or not they have undergone a ceremony of marriage.

A Modern Marriage

I was in conversation at a party with a man who was telling me about his partner and the beautiful marriage ceremony they had recently had. I had not been in the country very long, and was completely unaware of Danish marriage laws. "Is she here with you this evening?" I asked. He fixed me with a meaningful stare, and said, "Yes, he is standing over there." I concluded our conversation as gracefully as I could, and moved on, embarrassed, but wiser.

Some subjects, such as the right to life, are simply not issues in Denmark. Abortion has been legally available here since 1973. Permanent residents have the right to an abortion up to the twelfth week of gestation. This is an accepted fact among the vast majority of the population, and an opposing view would generally be seen as archaic and unenlightened.

Denmark was also the first country to legalize pornography in the late 1960s. Danish obscenity laws are few. They prohibit the selling of obscene pictures or objects to persons under the age of sixteen; the production, distribution, or ownership of obscene pictures or movies showing persons under the age of eighteen (though ownership of material showing a person between the ages of fifteen and eighteen is legal with their consent, as the Danish legal age of consent is fifteen); and obscene behavior in public.

There are no other pornography laws in Denmark, and pornography is freely available. Pornographic magazines and films can be found in most general stores. Visitors should also be aware that Danes are very open and frank when discussing their sexuality, sometimes to a point verging on the gynecological. To Danes, this is neither offensive nor a sign of attraction, so single travelers beware! Danish parents are also rather indulgent of their teenage sons' and daughters' sexual activities, and it is not unusual for a son or daughter to bring a partner home for the night.

Frankly Speaking
A Danish father complained at the breakfast table about the noise made by his son with his girlfriend the previous night. The son replied that since he had been listening to his mother and father most of his life he didn't think he had much ground for complaint!

GENDER EQUALITY

This is an equal-opportunity society, where equal rights are enshrined by law. Denmark's record on gender equality is impressive and there is little discrimination on the grounds of sex. There is a Ministry for Gender Equality, and 37.4 percent of members of parliament are women. Denmark is one of the countries with the highest proportion of women in the labor market. Danish women and men see and treat each other as equals. Some of the practical results of this may, however, be a little surprising to the visitor. Women should not expect the old-fashioned "hold the door and let the lady go first" treatment in Denmark. The door may well be held open by the person in front of you, but don't wait too long or it may swing back in your face.

Some women visitors complain about being jostled on Copenhagen's busier streets as men will not make way for them, especially if they are in a hurry. Women work in all branches of society, with the possible exception of waste disposal. Garbage men have remained garbage *men*. Some younger Danish women may take offense if a man gallantly stands aside to let them pass, but the usual reaction is one of momentary confusion and surprise. At the workplace Danish women do not seem to be as sensitive as their American counterparts, and there is a certain amount of sexual banter between men and women. It is, however, hard for the visitor to discern exactly where well-meaning jokes become harassment, and it is impossible, if not dangerous, to generalize in this area, so the visitor would be advised to leave that sort of thing to the locals.

Despite the legal position, in reality women are often disadvantaged. On average they earn 16 percent less than men, and there are fewer of them in senior positions. Women are more likely to leave work when a child is born, and this of course has repercussions on their career prospects.

Women are allowed four weeks' leave prior to giving birth, or more if necessary, and are obliged to take leave for the first two weeks after the birth. The full maternity entitlement is fourteen weeks after the birth, and the father is allowed two weeks' leave during this time, after which the parents are entitled to an additional thirty-two weeks' leave between them.

Both parents share the burden of raising their children. This is the natural consequence of the fact that in almost all Danish families both parents work. Much of the children's upbringing,

however, is left to the state in the form of day-care institutions, *vuggestue* (crèche) and *børnehave* (kindergarten), run by state-approved *pædagoger*.

PUNCTUALITY

Punctuality is important to Danes, and also for the foreign visitor, as the Danes are unlikely to make allowances for cultural diversity in this area. If you arrange to meet a Dane at one o'clock, then that does not mean five to one or five past one. As a rule of thumb, if you are going to be delayed for more than five minutes then call the person you are meeting and let them know. This will make things a lot easier.

Half an Hour to Twelve

One of the greatest sources of confusion in the area of timekeeping stems from some Danes' habit of translating directly from Danish to English while speaking. The source of this confusion is the Danish way of saying the time. If a Dane arranges to meet you at "half twelve" in the afternoon, and you arrive to find a rather irritated Scandinavian waiting for you (if he or she bothered to wait at all, that is), the explanation is quite simple.

When the Danes say "half twelve," they mean half an hour *to* twelve, and not half past, as has become the norm in the English-speaking world. They will also give the time as being, for example, "five minutes to half twelve" or "five minutes past half twelve."

On the Dot

My female colleague, who is English, told me about her Danish boyfriend's parents' rather endearing habit in this regard. In order to be punctual they would arrive early for dinner at the apartment she shared with him. They would then drive around the block, or stand outside, whatever the weather, waiting until the appointed time before ringing the doorbell to announce their arrival.

One result of this dedication to good timekeeping that you will soon notice is the punctuality of the public transportation services. As a rule, trains and buses arrive and depart on time and the slightest variation will be announced. In the business world good timekeeping is the norm. Danes will arrive at precisely the appointed time and expect the same from their foreign colleagues. The thinking behind this dedication to timekeeping can be traced to some of the values illustrated by the *Janteloven*. If you arrive early for an appointment then you will give the impression that you believe the person you are meeting is more important than you, or that your time is less valuable than theirs. If, on the other hand, you arrive late then you will give the impression that you are more important than the person you are meeting, or that your time is more valuable than theirs. Either way, this is in conflict with the "everyone is equal" spirit of the *Janteloven*.

KVALITETSBEVIDST (QUALITY AWARENESS)

During your visit to Denmark you may hear the term *kvalitetsbevidst* being used in relation to a person. The term is used to refer to someone who is conscious of the quality of the items they purchase and the services they use. The *kvalitetsbevidst* person is prepared to pay a little extra for something if he or she is sure that its quality is superior. If you live in a society that disapproves of ostentatious shows of wealth, then an insistence that your recently purchased expensive item was bought for its superior quality is a convenient excuse. It also saves you from any accusations of flouting the *Janteloven*. This expression has also been used ironically.

That is not to say that Danes don't like a bargain—quite the contrary. The average Dane will be only too delighted to tell you the price of his or her latest purchase if it was bought at a discount.

A remarkable amount of high-quality goods can be found in the average Danish apartment and designer furniture takes pride of place in Danish homes. Even when it comes to hobbies Danes remain *kvalitetsbevidst*: it is not unusual for a Danish cycle enthusiast to be found perched atop a horrendously expensive, carbon fiber, racing bike worthy of any Tour de France winner.

chapter three

CUSTOMS & TRADITIONS

PUBLIC HOLIDAYS AND FEAST DAYS

The Danes celebrate many important public holidays and feast days. On many of these occasions the Danish flag is flown from public buildings as well as from buses and private Danish homes. Public holidays are listed below.

January 1	New Year's Day
February/March	Fastelavn (Shrovetide)
March/April	Holy (Maundy) Thursday
March/April	Good Friday
March/April	Påske (Easter Day) Easter Monday
April/May	Stor Bededag (Great Prayer Day)
Middle/end May	Ascension Day
May/June	Pinse (Pentecost/Whit Sunday)
May/June	Pentecost/Whit Monday
June 5	Grundlovsdag (Constitution Day)
December 24	Juledag (Christmas Eve)
December 25	Christmas Day
December 26	Boxing Day

The following are the most important feasts and holidays.

Fastelavn (Shrovetide)

This is a feast for children. On the seventh Sunday before Easter Sunday they dress up in costume and take turns at tilting at a barrel. Originally there was a cat in the barrel, but in our more enlightened times the unfortunate animal has been replaced by sweets. It is believed that this tradition came from Dutch settlers in the Amager area of Copenhagen in the 1600s.

Påske (Easter)

Danes celebrate Easter in much the same way as it is celebrated in other countries, except that all flags are flown at half-mast until sunset. One unusual tradition is the sending of an anonymous letter in the shape of a snowdrop, bearing a poem that helps (or hinders) the receiver in guessing the identity of the sender. This is similar to a Valentine card—the Danes have not traditionally celebrated Valentine's Day until very recently, and still regard it as a mainly commercial invention for the benefit of florists and card manufacturers.

Stor Bededag (Great Prayer Day)

This observance, the fourth Friday after Easter, was introduced in 1686 to replace many other separate prayer and penitence days. Fasting was undertaken until the church service on the day itself. While the day remains an official holiday like many others, its religious significance is largely forgotten, but the tradition of eating hot muffins, *hveder,* continues.

Pinse (Pentecost/Whit Sunday)

On the Saturday before Pentecost/Whit Sunday it is traditional to go for a picnic in the woods. There are many events on this day, including carnivals in the major cities. Popular legend has it that the sun will dance on Whit Sunday morning, though there have been no confirmed sightings to date.

Grundlovsdag (Constitution Day)

On June 5 the Danes celebrate the introduction of the Constitution in 1849. Shops and schools are closed, and public institutions close at 12:00 noon. Quasi-political gatherings are held throughout the country, at which politicians make speeches and bands play music of all kinds. Families bring their children to these events, and there are picnics and a general party atmosphere. The largest of these gatherings takes place at Fælledparken in Copenhagen. Beer and other refreshments are available, including the inevitable selection of hotdogs.

St. Hans (Midsummer Day)

Originally a pagan festival celebrating the summer solstice, this day, June 24, is still celebrated in Denmark. The name, however, was changed to

St. Hans, or St. John's Day, with the advent of
Christianity in Denmark. In the evening bonfires
are lit around the country, and Midsummer's
Night speeches are made. Finally, the Midsummer
Night Song is sung to conclude events.

Mortens Aften (Martinmas)

This day, November 11, originally celebrated the
feast of St. Martin of Tours (336–97). Protestants
celebrate the birth of Martin Luther (1438–1546)
even though he was born on the previous day,
November 10. Traditionally, roast duck or goose
is eaten for dinner.

A Fair Roasting

The story is told that when St. Martin heard that the good citizens of Tours wanted to make him their bishop, he was reluctant to accept. To avoid their unwelcome approach he hid among the geese, but their cackling revealed his hiding place, and he was carried off by force. Many, therefore, feel that the goose deserves its Martinmas fate as traditional dish of the day.

Advent

The four Sundays before Christmas are marked by the lighting of candles on an Advent wreath. A candle is lit each Sunday, and small gifts are often exchanged. It is also traditional to drink mulled wine, called *glögg*, accompanied by *æbleskiver*, small batter cakes with sugar and jam.

Juledag (Christmas Eve)

Christmas Eve, December 24, is the major festival
of the year. Danes eat their traditional Christmas
dinner on Christmas Eve. The menu usually
consists of roast duck and pork with caramelized
and boiled potatoes, baked apple, and red cabbage.
This is followed by a cold rice pudding with cherry
sauce and chopped almonds. A whole almond is
hidden in the pudding, and the lucky finder wins
the "almond gift," traditionally a marzipan pig.
Afterward there is dancing around the Christmas
tree and the singing of traditional Christmas songs,
followed by the opening of presents.

A custom that the Danes have made their own
in the Christmas season is that of the Julefrokost,
or Christmas lunch. It is an informal occasion that
bears more resemblance to the medieval traditions
of the carnival than to a Christian feast. People have
the chance to let their hair down, drink too much,

and generally engage in activities that might at other times be frowned upon. These occasions are held by friends, families, and employers, and most Danes have a pretty hectic social calendar at this time of the year as a result.

THE DANES AND THEIR DRINKS

The Danish attitudes toward certain stimulants are in contrast to those of their Scandinavian brethren. The use of alcohol is an integral part of Danish life and is widely available, though expensive. The price of alcohol is a direct result of government policy to control the consumption of spirits, in particular, through taxation rather than by the more direct methods of other Scandinavian countries. As a result most Danes prefer to drink beer, which is cheaper, and a strong beer-drinking culture has taken root in Denmark. Traditionally

the favorite spirits of the Danish imbiber are *snaps*, made from potatoes, and Gammel Dansk, an aromatic, spicy liquor which is traditionally drunk at celebrations and family gatherings.

When it comes to drinking beer, Danes are in a class of their own. Nowadays, with the advent of the small microbreweries, there is a staggering range to choose from, including the impressive number of beers produced by Carlsberg and Tuborg. While many might regard these two giants of the brewing world as rivals they are, in fact, owned by the same company. They have contributed much to Danish cultural and scientific life, and evidence of this can be seen in buildings such as the Carlsberg Glypotek art museum on Hans Christian Andersen's Boulevard in Copenhagen. Danes expect others to hold their drink, and visitors would be well advised to pace themselves as the Danes do. The unfortunate

Swedes have for many years earned the gentle contempt of Danes for their excessive behavior on trips to Copenhagen.

Holding Your Own

One of the greatest tests of the drinking ability of the non-Dane is the *polterabent*, or stag/hen party. In Denmark these occasions usually last twenty-four hours, starting in the small hours of the morning. One that I personally attended lasted precisely that time, starting and finishing at 7:00 a.m.! Drink in Bacchanalian quantities is naturally a feature of such occasions.

Like most other EU countries Denmark introduced a ban on smoking in public places in 2007. Since then it has been illegal to smoke in restaurants, clubs, and public transport, as well as private and public workspaces. An exception was made, however, for bars smaller than 40 square meters. Smoking of electronic cigarettes, or vaping, has become increasingly popular in Denmark and vaping shops have sprung up throughout major towns and cities.

FAMILY CELEBRATIONS

There are many social and family gatherings to celebrate—important private events such as births, deaths, weddings, and anniversaries. Some are more celebrated than others. One such are the "round" birthdays—those ending with a zero, especially 50 and above. These are usually marked with a big party, and by the placing outside the celebrant's house of a large barrel painted with good wishes, as well as an announcement in the newspapers. Copper and silver wedding anniversaries are also occasions of note. In rural areas flags are flown not just by the happy couple but by their neighbors. Friends of the couple assemble outside the house in the early hours of the morning and, after placing an arch of branches over their door, serenade them outside their bedroom window. This is followed by a breakfast prepared by the couple for their "surprise" guests. Later on there may be a dinner, with songs, speeches, and plenty of drink.

Whatever the occasion, there are some customs and traditions of which the visitor should be aware, should he or she be lucky enough to be invited.

Introductions

On arrival, don't expect your host to introduce you to the company. Danes introduce themselves to each other, and will expect you to follow suit. This simply involves going around the company one by one, offering your hand and introducing yourself by your first name only. The Dane will then respond in kind, as should you when on the receiving end of this custom.

The Toast

Perhaps the most important tradition is the *skål*, or toast. Danes toast quite frequently on family occasions, and the toast takes a particular form. If you are giving the *skål*, you should pick up your glass and, catching the eye of someone else in the company, raise it to head height. Wait until everyone else who wants to has joined in and then raise the glass a little higher and say *skål,* pronounced "scoal," before drinking. It is always a good idea as well as good manners to *skål* one's host at a party, and it is the height of bad manners not to join in a *skål* when invited.

Singing is very popular at festive occasions, the songs usually having been composed by one of the guests to a popular or traditional melody. Given that most visitors to Denmark will not speak Danish and the songs are usually in that language, a rhythmical opening and closing of the mouth in the interests of solidarity is always a safe option! No Dane will expect you to attempt to sing in Danish.

THE PEOPLE'S CHURCH

While roughly 75 percent of Danish people belong to the Folkekirke, or "People's Church," an Evangelical Lutheran denomination, less than 5 percent are regular churchgoers. The Church is state-supported, with a minister in cabinet and government funding. The monarch or head of state is the only person in Denmark obliged to be a member of the Folkekirke. The Folkekirke has a special place in the Danish

constitution, the Grundlov. Article 4 of the Grundlov states that, "The Evangelical Lutheran Church shall be the Established Church, and as such shall be supported by the State." Article 66 states, "The constitution of the Established Church shall be laid down by statute." There exists therefore a unique official relationship between Church and state in Denmark. That said, however, the Church has very little relevance to Danes in their daily lives. It is said that the average Dane attends church four times—to be baptized, confirmed, married, and buried.

The Folkekirke is active in charitable work inside and outside Denmark by way of of its charitable organization, Folkekirkens Nødhjælp. Other than through such charitable works the Folkekirke plays a purely ceremonial role in Danish life. While the majority of Danes would regard themselves as Christian in spirit, there is little evidence of this so far as practicing their religion goes.

chapter four

MAKING FRIENDS

The Danes generally are polite, friendly people who are easy to get along with. Becoming accepted as an outsider is relatively easy. Denmark is a multicultural society, and Danes both welcome and are interested in meeting foreigners. Indeed, it is sometimes easier to meet people as a foreigner in Denmark than as

a native. As long as one is prepared for the Danish characteristic of straight talking there should not be any problems. While Danes willingly discuss any subject under the sun with an acquaintance, they are loath to reveal their deeper personal feelings and are not given to shows of emotion. These are reserved for conversations with good friends, and should a Dane be forthcoming in this area it can be taken as a sign of trust and friendship.

Becoming close friends with a Dane is something that requires both time and patience. Danes value their friends highly, and maintain contact with them. Although they may have a wide circle of acquaintances and work colleagues with whom they socialize, their circle of intimate friends is usually much smaller. Most close friendships go back a very long way, many stemming from childhood, or school or university days, and while some friendships may have come about through work, this is usually the exception. Danes have a tendency to function best in groups, even while socializing, and they enjoy meeting people in clubs, for example. They are not generally very comfortable meeting someone new outside a group setting, and it is therefore very unusual to be approached by a Dane.

To be close friends with a Dane in Denmark does require one essential ingredient, and that is knowledge of the language. Although most

Danes speak English, it may well be rather a strain for them to speak it over a long period of time, and this can put a brake on the progress of a friendship. Learning Danish is a worthwhile exercise, as once you become friends with a Dane you really do have a friend for life.

ENTERTAINING

While Danes do "go out on the town," they tend to do most of their entertaining at home, mainly due to the cost of entertaining out. One only has to walk down one of Copenhagen's residential streets on a weekend to hear the sounds of music and parties coming from the open windows. In the summer months the barbecue has become a favored form of entertainment among those lucky enough to have a garden. Private parties are usually very relaxed

occasions. Dress is casual, and it is customary
to bring some beer or a bottle of wine.

If you are invited to dinner then it will usually
be at your Danish host's home. The evening meal
usually takes place between 6:00 and 8:00 p.m.
If you wish to bring a present with you, then a
bottle of wine, flowers, or chocolates would be
appropriate. Typically you will be ushered straight
to the dinner table. Your host and hostess will
probably sit at opposite ends of the table, with
the female guest of honor seated to the right of
the host and the male to the right of the hostess.
Many toasts, or *skål*, will be drunk.

If the menu is traditional then the meal will
consist of three courses: a fish or seafood appetizer,
a main meat course with salad, and dessert.
There will be bread on the table, and wine with
all courses. A note on etiquette: eating in the

American style, cutting up your food first and then putting down your knife to eat just with your fork, is considered childish by most Europeans, Danes included. Use both knife and fork, to cut and eat in the European manner.

After the meal there will be drinks and conversation. Danish dinners can last up to five or six hours so you can expect to be at the table for a while! It is not customary to rise before your host and hostess do.

INTRODUCING . . . YOURSELF!

Introductions in Denmark tend to be something one does for oneself, rather than waiting for a third party to perform them for you. At parties and social gatherings you do a round of the room, shaking everyone by the hand, looking them in the eye, and introducing yourself by your first name. They will respond in a similar fashion. The best approach on first meetings is, therefore, to take the initiative and introduce yourself to those you meet, avoiding any long conversations that might hinder the process for others until all the guests have arrived. When leaving, again, take the initiative and say good-bye to each person in turn. While this may seem unnecessary at a large gathering, the Danes don't try to slip out unnoticed—it's simply bad form.

Should you call a company and be answered by a receptionist, she or he may not apologize for the fact that the person you are trying to contact is not there, saying something like "Mr. Bendtsen is not in the office" instead of the English, "I'm sorry Mr. Bendtsen is not in the office at the moment." This is not rudeness—Danes do not understand why they should apologize for something that is beyond their control, or for a simple fact. On the telephone people will introduce themselves by saying, "*Det er . . .*," followed by their name. This means, literally translated, "It's . . .," and they may also do this in English. They will not expect this of non-Danes.

SOCIALIZING, AT WORK AND AFTER WORK

The Danes are the most social Scandinavians. They are easy to start a conversation with and

always ready to discuss any topic. They do have a penchant for compartmentalizing their lives, however, and everything has a time and a place. There is a clear line drawn between the private and the working spheres, and in the workplace Danes tend to socialize very little. Also, of course, time is usually at a premium at the workplace. Tasks have to be completed and deadlines met, and there is no room for social chitchat. A side effect of this is that when it comes to business negotiations the Danes tend to get down to it very quickly, with as little time spent on introductions as possible. The idea of relationship-building as part of the negotiations is entirely alien to them.

The long, leisurely lunch break is also an alien concept to Danes, as is the idea of a working lunch. Most people will bring a *madpakke*, or packed lunch, to work, and will hastily consume it during the half-hour break. Sometimes they will have lunch out of the office, but this is usually only when entertaining clients. Many will simply eat lunch on the move if they have to go from one place to another during the working day—it is not unusual to see someone hurrying along a street in Copenhagen with a briefcase in one hand and a sandwich in the other.

The short lunch break is leisure time for the Danes, and many of them regard it as sacrosanct, and not a time to discuss matters relating to work. Try not to telephone Danish workers during their lunch break, unless you are calling on an entirely non-work-related matter. They may not bawl you out, but they are unlikely to be pleased with you for interrupting their precious leisure time. You are disrupting the *hygge* of their lunch break (see page 95).

Danes socialize little after work unless it is a social function organized by their workplace. If this is the case then spouses will not come unless they also work for the same firm. Danes maintain a very strict divide between their work and social lives and rarely mix the two.

WHAT SHOULD I WEAR?

Modesty and "fitting in" are the alpha and omega of the Danish dress code, and of course this can cause difficulties for the visitor. The Danes are generally informal, but on social occasions you should dress according to both the occasion and the venue. You do not attend your new Danish friend's silver wedding anniversary in old jeans and sneakers.

The Danes have pretty much eliminated the class system, and dress cannot be taken as an indication of social or professional status. (Among certain segments of society a sort of color coding exists. Gardeners, for example, wear green or brown overalls, while painters and bricklayers wear white. Most manual workers wear blue overalls, the exception being those who wear a corporate uniform, such as the red uniform of Copenhagen Energy, for example.)

In the office environment Danes tend to be relaxed in their attire. As long as you look smart and tidy, you should be all right. Business suits are usually worn when meeting representatives from foreign companies, although many Danish businessmen eschew a shirt and tie in favor of either an open-necked shirt or a dark-colored polo-necked sweater.

The one area in which dress codes do not seem to exist is in the wearing of hats in winter. Walking along the streets of most of the larger cities in Denmark, you will be surprised by the sheer variety of headgear worn, not all of it very smart or fashionable! Most hats will cover the ears, protecting them from the cold and the strong winds Denmark experiences in winter. On a practical note, this is a point that should not be missed by the winter visitor—uncovered ears in winter quickly lead to a headache.

SOCIETIES AND ASSOCIATIONS

Danes in general like things to be organized. It is no surprise, therefore, that they like nothing better than to be members of clubs, societies, and associations. No matter how obscure your

interests or hobbies, there is a good chance
that there is an association for it in Denmark.
Contacting these groups is also an excellent way
for foreigners to meet and converse with Danes in
a relaxed, social atmosphere. Many organizations
have Web sites with sections in English.

chapter five

THE DANES AT HOME

THE DANISH HOME

While the Englishman views his home as his castle, the Dane views his home as his cave—a warm, comfortable place that offers escape from the pressures and stress of the outside world. One has only to consider the amount of time Danes spend in their homes during the long, dark Scandinavian winters to realize the importance of the home in Danish family life.

In the cities most people live in apartment buildings, many of which are arranged around a quadrangle with a central, green, common area. Apartments in Denmark fall into three main categories. First there is the *ejerlejlighed*, or owned apartment. Second, there is the rented apartment. Between these two is the *andelslejlighed*, which is an apartment in a building owned under a cooperative or multi-ownership scheme. The purchasers pay a large upfront sum for a share in the building, and then pay a reduced rent every month, which will usually include heat and other services.

As rents are controlled in Denmark, rented property is reasonably cheap when compared with property in other European countries with similar standards of living. In the cities, however, property is at a premium, so long-term visitors should plan well ahead. There are many relocation firms to help with acquiring property and take care of the details.

HYGGE—THE DANISH COMFORT ZONE

An important term that is always associated with, among other things, the home, is *hygge*, or *hyggeligt*. It is very difficult to do the term justice in English, most commentators being satisfied with "cozy." This is, however an inadequate translation as it does not encompass the scope of the word, which can be used to describe people, situations, and locations. The term *hygge* conveys, to a Dane, ideas such as intimacy, relaxation, hospitality, warmth, friendliness, geniality, harmony, and contentment, to name but a few. Perhaps one approach would be

to think of it as anything that conveys the feeling one had, as a child, when getting a warm hug from a loving parent.

Comfort in Court

A friend of mine, a Danish lawyer, once told me a story about his own experience of *hygge*. He was cross-examining a witness in court, and as he felt the witness was resisting he became more insistent with his questioning. After a short while the trial judge recessed the hearing and asked my friend to join him in his chambers for a chat. He then gently admonished him for being too aggressive with the witness as he felt it was disrupting the *hygge* of his court!

A Dane's home should, first and foremost, be a *hyggelig* place to be. This is the ideal that all Danes strive to attain. Danish houses and apartment buildings are, therefore, extremely well-insulated, with double-glazed windows and excellent heating systems. Candles are used in abundance to create an atmosphere of *hygge*, not just at home but also in restaurants and cafés.

DANISH DESIGN

Classic Danish design is beautiful; but whatever the aesthetic qualities, beauty has not been the primary aim of the designers. In Denmark, design is typically regarded as a problem-solving process. A designer works to solve a problem in the simplest way, without violating the complexity of the task or forgetting that a new design must,

above all, be functional. These criteria are the basis of Danish design. The solution to the task should be as simple and natural as possible, while respecting the requirements of cost and environment. The aim is to create collaboration between the user and the object, which therefore must be easy to use as well as aesthetically pleasing. Given this background, it is obvious that the essence of Danish design is neither style nor fashion, but the expression and result of a set of aims and values on the part of the designer. This approach has led to items of simple beauty with clean, flowing lines and an absence of decoration.

Original examples of Danish design are, however, extremely expensive and therefore many Danish homes abound with the products of that well-known Swedish concern, Ikea. This is mainly due to the fact that, for Danes, the combination of Scandinavian design and cheap prices is extremely enticing. Most Danes, though, will make an effort to have something from a well-known Danish designer in their homes, justifying the outlay on the grounds of *kvalitet,* lest they be accused of a fundamental breach of the dreaded *Jantelov.*

LEAVE YOUR SHOES AT THE DOOR

Danes remove their shoes before entering each other's homes, and there are two reasons for this. First, it avoids dragging dirt from outside all over their host's home. Second, most Danish homes

make extensive use of wood flooring, which high or hard heels could damage with dents or unsightly marks. Many people bring soft indoor shoes to change into when visiting each other.

Don't expect to be given a grand tour of the residence. Danes are by nature private people, and their home is the center of their private world. Remain in the room you are taken into. If your hosts want you to see other rooms they will clearly invite you to do so. Never go wandering around the house unbidden, as it is highly unlikely that you would be invited again.

The visitor may notice some unusual features. For example, most kitchens have two garbage bins, a black and a green, usually located in the cupboard under the sink. The black bin is for ordinary garbage and the green is for recyclable items. Another surprise may await you in the bathroom. Many homes use the Scandinavian shower system, owing to the confines of space. Basically the bathroom *is* the shower, with a sealed floor sloping down to a drainage hole. When taking a shower you pull the shower curtain around to avoid splashing the rest of the room.

BIG BROTHER IS WATCHING OVER YOU

Denmark is famous for its cradle-to-grave health-care service. The state is ever present in the life of Danes, from the moment they are born to the moment of their death. The vast majority of Danes are born in a state hospital, where mother and baby are cared for at the state's expense. The state also provides, by way of generous maternity and paternity provisions, ample opportunity for both parents to spend time with their child.

From six months children may be sent to a *vuggestue*, or day-care center, where they will be looked after while the parents are at work. At the age of three they will be moved to a *børnehave*, or kindergarten, until they start school at the age of six. Both of these institutions are partially state-subsidized. There has been some debate in Denmark about this scheme, as many feel that children become rather institutionalized. Certainly there is little doubt that the state child-care system contributes largely to the homogenization of values and attitudes in Danish society.

Danish children begin school proper at the age of six, either in one of the state *folkeskoler* or in one of the many private schools around the country, where they will receive their primary and lower secondary education up to the age of sixteen. This course of education is compulsory for all Danes. Should parents choose to send their children to a private school, they pay only the difference in fees between those of the private school and the cost of attending a state school, the balance being paid directly to the school by the state. After leaving the *folkeskole* students can choose to continue their education at the upper secondary level by attending either a *gymnasium* or a vocational education and

LIFELONG LEARNING

One interesting aspect of education in Denmark is the enthusiasm for "lifelong learning." This idea stems from the *folkeoplysning*, or "popular enlightenment" ideas of the Danish educator Grundtvig. The purpose of this learning is the interpretation and exploration of the meaning of life. Teaching is of a general educational nature, which should not be dominated by individual subjects, and courses do not lead to examinations. These courses are funded by the state through local authorities. Courses are run through night schools, and sports and youth associations and clubs.

The fundamental principles of popular enlightenment are free choice of topics, universal access, free initiative, and free choice of teachers. In rural areas special "People's High Schools" provide this type of education. These schools are residential and in general participants are expected to help with the daily chores of cooking, washing, and cleaning up. The schools are self governing institutions and are subsidized by the state on the basis of the number of pupils attending.

training institution until the age of nineteen or so. Qualifying from *gymnasium* is an important family and social occasion, with a graduation ceremony followed by a party with one's classmates. One tradition is for the newly graduated class to tour their local area on a flatbed truck or a horse-drawn trailer suitably decorated for the occasion. They then visit the home of each class member, where they receive food and drink before being sent on their less than sober way to the next destination.

The Danish student then has the choice of going on either to university or to another form of higher education. Should they choose to do so, they will be supported by the state by the SU, a monthly grant for living expenses while they are studying. All Danes are eligible for this grant, which is not means tested. It should be noted that the ages given above are the theoretical minimum ages for formal courses of education. Danish pupils are usually older due to sabbaticals or change of study programs, among other things.

MILITARY SERVICE

For Danish males, however, there is one event that can interrupt this educational progression: military service. Under Section 81 of the Danish Constitution all Danish males are liable for military service from the age of eighteen. Should they be called up they will be subject to both mental and physical examinations before being approved for service. Their period of service is for up to fourteen months. Should a conscript have to leave a job to perform military service, that job must, under Danish law, be held open for his return once he has completed his service. Military service can be postponed until education is completed.

THE TIES THAT BIND—MARRIAGE

At some stage in their lives Danes may want to marry and settle down. While the ceremonies and receptions are not as large and lavish as they might be in the USA, marriage is regarded as a big step, and treated as one of the major family celebrations. Denmark was the first country in the world to recognize same-sex partnerships in 1989, giving them equal legal status with heterosexual married couples. The Folkekirke, however, does not recognize such unions.

There are some traditions in Danish weddings that a guest may like to be aware of. Before the wedding a gate of honor—an arch of pine branches—is made in front of the bride's home. On the wedding day, during the reception, the groom will leave the room, and this is the cue for all the male guests to form a line and kiss the bride. When the groom returns the bride will leave the room and the female guests will line up to kiss the groom. The bride and groom will also kiss once above the table, usually standing on a chair, and once below the table. This is usually accompanied by the guests stamping their feet in unison on the floor. When all the guests tap their glasses, the newly weds must again kiss! If just one person taps his or her glass, this is for silence, and he or she will make a speech. At some point after the meal the guests will gather around the groom, and a pair of scissors will be used to relieve him of his socks and tie. The wedding waltz is a traditional song to which the bride and groom dance, encircled by their wedding guests. As the dance continues the guests slowly tighten the circle until the bride and groom can no longer dance. This must be performed before midnight.

The traditional Danish wedding cake is a marzipan ring cake, also known as a cornucopia, elaborately decorated with sugar work. It is filled with fresh fruit, candy, and almond cakes. The cake is cut by the bride and groom together and all the guests eat a piece to ward off bad luck.

Of course not all Danes marry; many people simply cohabit. We have seen that, when speaking English, cohabiters habitually refer to their partner as their wife or husband, so one shouldn't take this as an indicator of legal status.

HOME SWEET HOME

Housing in Danish cities is expensive, and most city dwellers live in apartment blocks. In the suburbs the housing estate, or *villakvarter*, is the most popular form of housing. There has been another sharp rise in the price of housing in Denmark in recent years, following the economic turbulence of 2008, when prices fell dramatically. The cost of housing today means that in most Danish families there is no longer a choice regarding both parents working. Additionally, while there is often a sharp difference in house prices between urban and rural areas, popular coastal

areas near large cities like Copenhagen are almost on a par with the city.

SHOPPING

Danes like value for money, and this is reflected in their shopping habits. Most people do their daily shopping at large budget supermarket chains, such as Netto and the German-owned Aldi, both of which have a no-frills, value-for-money approach. Service is minimal to keep overheads down and, thereby, prices. The upper end of the market would be represented by the Irma chain, but fewer Danes will go there for shopping on a daily basis, preferring to use them for the purchase of luxury foods. Service in Danish supermarkets is in general below the standards of the USA, due to the high cost of wages and the need to keep overheads down in a competitive market.

The visitor should be aware that cutting in the line at any Danish store is likely to result in an argument with an outraged Dane. One patiently waits one's turn in Denmark.

Shopping hours used to be controlled by legislation. On October 1, 2012, the Danish government changed the law on opening hours to allow shops to open 24/7 if they wish, except on public holidays and after 3:00 p.m. on Christmas Eve and New year's Eve. Shops with a turnover of less than 32.2 million Danish kr., about US $5 million, are allowed to open every day of the year.

WORK

The Dane, we've seen, has two lives: work and home. The two do not necessarily meet, as many people maintain a strict division between their working life and their leisure. Office hours in Denmark are from 8:00 a.m. to 4:00 p.m. As most child-care facilities close at 5:00 p.m., parents prefer to avoid staying late at work if possible. However, many Danes do have the possibility of working from home for part of the time, and others may take some work home to do after the children are in bed.

For the majority of Danes the working day starts at 8:00 a.m. and finishes between 4:00 and 5:00 p.m. with a thirty-minute lunch break, usually at 12:00 noon. Most businesses also have short coffee breaks of about fifteen minutes at around 10:00 a.m. In Denmark a full working week is thirty-seven hours, and while paid overtime is rare it is not unheard of. All Danish workers are entitled to five weeks' paid vacation. Holiday entitlements are regulated by the Holidays With Pay Act, and as a result it is illegal to make an agreement for less holiday time. Under the Act all employees are entitled to take three weeks of continuous vacation between May 1 and September 30. The vacation time remaining can be taken at any time during the year but must be of at least five days' duration.

Parents are entitled to a total of fifty-two weeks' maternity/paternity leave. The mother can take leave four weeks before the birth and fourteen weeks after. The father is entitled to two weeks' leave during the first fourteen weeks after the birth of the child. The parents can then decide between themselves how they will take the remaining thirty-two weeks. Couples who adopt a baby are entitled to a total of forty-eight weeks' leave after receiving the child. Should a child fall ill, then the parents can take the first day of the child's illness off with full pay.

By law all employees must receive a contract within one month of starting employment, covering conditions of salary, including payment during periods of maternity leave, illness, and vacation; seniority bonuses and commissions; pension; working hours; vacations; period of notice; overtime payment; definition of working sphere; and clear job title. Generally, after three months' probationary period, employees are entitled to be given three months' notice of dismissal. Employees, on the other hand, need only give one month's notice of their intention to leave.

A TYPICAL DAY

The Danes rise early—they have to if children are to be delivered to day care and school and adults are to be at work by 8:00 a.m. Breakfast consists of either cereal or oatmeal porridge, and/or bread and butter with various cold toppings such as meat or cheese, and coffee, tea, or fruit juice. The children are then taken to their day-care centers, which open at 6:00 a.m. and can if necessary provide breakfast for their young charges. Older children have to be at school by 8:00 a.m.

Many Danes, adults and children, take packed lunches. The children have to be collected by 6:00 p.m. from their day-care centers, or after-school centers for the older children, where they can participate in various pursuits under supervision. Dinner is usually eaten between 5:00 and 7:00 p.m., and is an important family occasion when the day's events can be discussed. After dinner there are a few hours of leisure time before lunch packs are prepared for the following day, and everyone is in bed early on weekdays, ready to repeat the process the following day.

A VERY SMALL HOUSE IN THE COUNTRY

One great Danish family tradition that should not go unmentioned is that of the summerhouse. Danes like to take their family summer vacation in Denmark. It saves travel costs, everyone speaks Danish, and they get a chance to enjoy the pure, unspoiled countryside. To this purpose many Danes invest in a *sommerhus*, or summerhouse. These are typically made from wood, small in size, with a small garden attached. Summerhouses have a special status under Danish law and are only partially taxed. As such, foreigners are not allowed to buy summerhouses. They are normally lived in for only a few weeks and shut up for the rest of the year. Complexes of summerhouses can be seen at most of Denmark's popular vacation spots.

chapter six

TIME OUT

The most outgoing of Scandinavians, the Danes enjoy the company of friends and acquaintances, and like to meet new people. It is worth remembering that they respect privacy, and therefore it is up to you, the visitor, to introduce yourself to people, as otherwise they will assume that you want to be left alone. This is not a daunting prospect as a visitor, in particular a foreign one, will usually be made welcome.

Danes regard drink as a source of social lubrication. Beer is the alcohol of choice in the nation that claims it produces the best lager in the world. Most bars and cafés have a reasonable selection of beers, with Carlsberg and Tuborg being the favorites. Public drunkenness is condoned, as long as it stays within the limits of propriety. Danes are especially accepting, if not indulgent, of drunkenness among foreigners, with the possible exception of Swedes. They do not, however, tolerate drunk driving or any other breach of the law resulting from overindulgence, and a visitor will receive no sympathy from their Danish friends, the public, or the authorities in such a case.

HERE COMES THE SUN
Coming as they do from a cold northern climate, it is no surprise that sunny, warm destinations

are a favorite among the vacationing Danes.
Every summer Danish cars towing trailers
and camping vehicles can be seen crossing
the border like herds of migrating wildebeest
in search of sunnier climes to the south.
During the winter vacations travel agents do a
brisk trade, sending Danes off to more exotic
destinations in their quest for some winter sun.
Skiing holidays are also popular, particularly
in Sweden, France, and Austria.

SERVICE

Danish service, while being good by Scandinavian
standards, is not up to American standards.
Many visitors are surprised at the lack of
rapport between staff and customers in Danish
businesses. You should remember that you are
in a country that stresses equality, and therefore
people have a natural aversion to anything that
implies servitude. Service is usually therefore
efficient if somewhat lacking in the friendliness
that Americans may be used to at home.

BANKS AND CURRENCY EXCHANGE

The Danish krone is the unit of currency. Most
twenty-four-hour ATMs in Denmark accept most
credit cards and have menus available in English.
Banks are open in Denmark from 10:00 a.m. to
4:00 p.m., Monday to Friday, and until 5:00 p.m.

on Thursdays. All banks are closed on weekends and public holidays. Banks have a ticket system for those waiting for service. Simply press the button marked *kasse*, take a numbered ticket for the teller, and wait your turn.

Credit cards are accepted at most stores, but don't take a Visa sign as an assurance that the store will accept your card. Some stores only accept Danish Visa cards, so check this before you make a purchase. American Express cards are accepted at some stores. A few stores may accept traveler's checks, but most do not, and you may find yourself having to cash these at a bank.

EATING OUT

Cafés offer alcohol, coffee, tea, and food throughout the day. Bars may serve coffee if requested, but

they mainly serve alcohol, and rarely have food. Not surprisingly, pork is the national dish of Denmark, and can be found in all its glorious variations in restaurants throughout the country. In the larger cities restaurants serve both traditional Danish as well as a wide variety of international cuisine. You may have a problem if you wish to order something that differs even slightly from what is written on the menu. Many establishments tend to be rather pedantic about this, and basically you can order only what's on the menu exactly as it is described.

TIPPING

The minimum wage ensures that nobody has to rely on tips to make a living, and tipping is neither usual nor expected. Most bars, restaurants, and cafés add a service charge of 15 percent. Danes therefore only tip waiting and hotel staff if the service has been particularly good. If you feel that the service deserves it, then a tip in the region of 10–15 percent of the final bill would be appropriate, or you could simply round up the check.

Most Danish restaurants and cafés are child friendly. Many will produce high chairs on request. As far as children's behavior is concerned, you should use your own common sense—for instance, don't let your children run around where they can get under the feet of people carrying hot food to the tables.

ADONIS THE DANE: HEALTH AND FITNESS

Walk down any street in Denmark and you will soon notice that, as a nation, the Danish people are in pretty good shape. Fitness clubs do a brisk trade and there are plenty of joggers. It may strike the visitor as unusual then that the Danes are so liberal when it comes to issues such as smoking and drinking. It is not unusual to see a fit-looking young man or woman come out of the gym, stop, and light a cigarette before continuing down the street with their gym bag slung over their shoulder. A possible explanation for this may be that many Danes simply do not see why, given that they smoke, they should let the rest of their physical regimen fall by the wayside. Another explanation may be that they are interested merely in looking good.

Danes are careful about what they put into their bodies. Organic produce is available in most of the major chain supermarkets, and is most popular with city dwellers. It is marked and rated by the Department for Agriculture and Food and is then given the "Ø" mark for "Økologisk," meaning that it is certified by the government to be genuinely organic produce.

The Danes rank among the most pro-organic consumers in the world. The sale of organic food makes up 13.3 percent of the total food market in Denmark—the highest of any country. At 51.4 percent, more than half the Danish population buy organic food every week.

NATIONAL SPORTS AND PASTIMES

Two sports dominate Danish television ratings: soccer and handball. Soccer is both played and watched widely in Denmark. The domestic game is dominated by two sides—FC Copenhagen, and Brondby—both based in the greater Copenhagen city area. Internationally, while not again reaching the heights of their European Championship victory in 1984, the international soccer team has always performed respectably in international competitions. Many Danish players play with some of the biggest European and English clubs. The Danish handball team is dominant in that sport. Both the male and female handball teams have won at world championship and Olympic levels.

Denmark is a cycling nation, and Danes have also been successful in the cycling world. A Danish team, CSC, won the team section of the famous Tour de France. The manager of that team, Bjarne Riis, was himself a former Tour de France winner.

CULTURE, HIGH AND LOW

The Royal Danish Ballet is one of the best ballet companies in the world, and regularly produces world-class interpretations of the classical ballets as well as more modern pieces at its home in the Royal Theatre on Kongens Nytorv in the center of Copenhagen. Going to the ballet in Copenhagen has less of the pomp and circumstance than one might expect, as the *Jantelov* applies to the world of the arts as much as it does to any other aspect of Danish society. The dress code is not strict, though neat and tidy dress is recommended.

In general, Danes do not associate high culture with any particular social group, as is

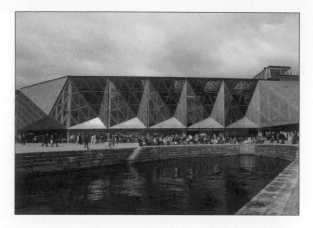

the case in many other countries. Anyone can go to the ballet or opera—there is a modern opera house in Copenhagen—and ticket prices are reasonable. Booking ahead for many of the more popular productions is recommended.

The Louisiana Museum of Modern Art is famous for its important collection of sculptures, paintings, and programs of special exhibitions. Perched on the shore at the Øresund Sound, it is worth a visit for the setting alone. Only half an hour by train from central Copenhagen, this particularly Danish synthesis of art, architecture, and nature makes for an unmissable day trip.

Festivals
There are many popular music festivals in Denmark, although by far the largest and best-

known of them is the Roskilde Festival, held in
July of every year. This is in fact the largest rock
festival in Scandinavia. It draws top international
acts, lasts over a week, and people come from
all over Europe, pitching their tents in the
camping areas provided. It received some bad
press in the past when a tragic accident led to the
deaths of some fans as a result of crushing, due
to the press of the crowd. Security procedures
were updated and the festival has gone from
strength to strength, attracting top national and
international acts.

The Copenhagen Jazz Festival takes place
in the first two weeks of July, and is one of the
leading jazz events in Scandinavia. During the
festival jazz is played in venues around the city
as well as on the streets.

Live music is very popular in most of Denmark's major cities, and you should not have a problem finding a venue whether your taste is pop, rock, jazz, or country and western.

Film

The Danish Film Industry is state-supported. As Danish is such a relatively little-spoken language, the industry simply could not exist without state support in the form of grants and funding. Denmark has had a few notable successes on the international film scene, with Lars von Trier being perhaps the best-known Danish director today. He was one of a group of Danish directors who formed the "dogma" movement, a dominant force in modern Danish filmmaking. To have a film officially certified as a "dogma" film there must be no use of artificial lighting, no use of special effects, including background music, and the actors must wear their own clothes. While quite popular in Denmark, the movement hasn't really caught on outside the country.

More recently Danish TV series have become very popular abroad: the rights to series such as "The Killing" have been bought by large American TV production companies with a view to remaking their own versions. In the UK the popularity of Danish and Swedish series has led to the creation of new, if unofficial, genres called Scandi-Crime and Scandi-Drama.

Comic Books

In many homes you may notice a collection of comics on the bookshelves. Comics have always been popular in Denmark, particularly graphic novels, and many are translated for the Danish market. Denmark also produces titles of its own, and collectors give their favorite titles pride of place on their bookshelves. Many of these comics are written for the adult market, with quite complex storylines and advanced language that most children would find hard to understand. Some are for the very adult market, being pornographic in nature. In fact, one of Denmark's leading porn magazines also brings out a monthly comic book version for aficionados. Of the more mainstream comics the storylines are wide and diverse, ranging from Westerns to historical stories to science fiction. The Japanese manga-style comic book is also very popular.

chapter seven

TRAVEL, HEALTH & SAFETY

As Denmark is such a small country traveling around it is relatively easy, as most distances are extremely short in comparison with American standards. At no time, for instance, can you be more than about 25 miles (40 kilometers) from the coast in Denmark. Flying is quick and easy. The road and rail networks are extensive and in good repair. As most Danes speak reasonably good English most of the usual pitfalls with regard to timetables and ticket purchases can be avoided. When traveling, Danes tend to keep to themselves, and therefore there may not be the same opportunities to converse with the locals that you may have in other countries. There can be a little pushing and shoving getting on and off public transportation, but this is usually because people are in a hurry to get going. To take this sort of behavior as a personal offense would be a misinterpretation.

PUBLIC TRANSPORTATION

The rail network in Denmark is extensive, reliable, frequent, and relatively cheap. All Denmark's

major cities are connected by rail. Almost all of the
train services are run by the Danish State Railway
Service, DSB.

The intercity trains are modern, comfortable,
and have both first- and second-class cars. It is
necessary to make a reservation on these trains.
Cars are roomy, and the seating arrangements
usually consist of two pairs of seats, facing each
other across a table. The trains also have play areas
for small children, restrooms with diaper-changing
facilities, and power outlets for laptop computers
and other electronic equipment.

Interregional trains are similar, and although
you are not required to make a reservation on
these, it would be sensible to do so at busy times
o ensure a seat. Most intercity and interregional
trains run on an hourly basis.

In the cities and towns, with the exception of
Copenhagen which has a comprehensive train and

metro system, buses are the main form of public
transportation. Again, services are efficient and
punctual. You can buy your tickets at the central
bus station or any of the main train stations. In
and around Copenhagen you can skip lines and
avoid credit card foreign transaction fees by
purchasing tickets through the free smartphone
app Mobilbilleter. Click on "*Indstillinger*" to
change the language from Danish to English.

In Copenhagen many commuters use an
electronic traveling card called "Rejsekort"
and at all train stations in the city as well as on
buses you will see the blue half spheres used by
commuters to check in and check out with their
travel card. All public transportation in Denmark
is wheelchair friendly, and employees are only too
happy to help disabled passengers with boarding
or disembarkation if necessary. There is usually a

button near the exit with a wheelchair symbol over it, which you can press for assistance.

The capital city, Copenhagen, has an internal train system known as the *S-Tog*, or S-Train. The trains run between most areas of Copenhagen on a regular basis, usually every five to ten minutes. Complementing this service is the Metro, or subway, service. The Metro service is limited but expanding. Tickets and information on both services can be obtained from any DSB office at most train stations.

RENTING A CAR

The Danish road network is extensive, with expressways running between all the major towns and cities. Traffic is rarely gridlocked, even in the major cities, although congestion will be experienced during the rush hour, usually

between 6:00 and 9:00 a.m. and between 3:00 and
5:00 p.m. All the islands that make up Denmark
are connected by ferry services or bridges, some
of which are toll bridges.

Renting a car can be expensive in Denmark in
comparison with neighbouring Germany, so if your
trip is starting in Germany you might consider
renting your vehicle there and driving to Denmark.
All the major car rental companies have offices in
Copenhagen so booking through them could be one
way of saving money. In Denmark, as in the USA,
you drive on the right-hand side of the road. Danes
are not the most tolerant of motorists and expect
other drivers to be aware of the rules of the road. As
rental cars in Denmark do not have any special plates
indicating they are rental cars you can expect the
occasional episode of horn blowing!

You must drive with low-beam headlights on
at all times. These come on automatically in most
rental cars, but it may be worth checking that this
is the case. The wearing of seat belts is mandatory,
and children under 135 cm (4 ft. 5 in.) must use
an approved safety seating device adapted to their
height and weight. Distances and speed limits are
given in metric kilometers, so the general speed
limits are, for example, 50 kmph (31 mph) in built-
up areas, 80 kmph (49.7 mph) on major roads,
and either 110 or 130 kmph (68 or 80 mph) on
expressways. Fines for speeding vary according to
the percentage by which you exceed the speed limit,
and can be collected on the spot. Danish drivers

are very bad at keeping within the speed limits, especially on expressways, but this has changed somewhat with the introduction of the new 130 kmph limit on some expressways.

Although Denmark is the home of Carlsberg beer, and Danes in general love their beer, they are very responsible when it comes to driving and alcohol. The permitted limit is 0.08 percent. Driving under the influence of alcohol is penalized stiffly in Denmark, and there is no public sympathy for the offender. Attempting to drive while drunk will be regarded as stupid.

Parking in the major cities and towns is operated on a "pay and display" system. A kerb-side vending machine is used to purchase tickets or they can be purchased electronically with the EasyPark smartphone app. For any further information on driving in Denmark, contact the Danish motoring organization, the FDM, or look up their Web site on the Internet: www.fdm.dk.

Should you be unfortunate enough to be involved in an accident, do not move your vehicle until the police arrive, unless its position constitutes a serious danger to other road users. Should you have to move it, it would be a good idea to take photographs of it at the accident site before doing so. The Danish police are generally very helpful to tourists, and speak English to at least a reasonable standard. It is an offense in Denmark to drive a vehicle without having your license physically with you, so keep it safely on hand in the car.

TAXIS

Most of the major towns and cities have a taxi service. You can hail a cab in the street if it has its *fri* sign lit, or find one at a stand. Alternatively you can order one by calling a taxi company, such as Copenhagen-based 4x35, helpfully named after their phone number, (+45) 35 35 35 35. Be aware that there is a booking charge, however. Taxi app Uber ceased operations in Denmark in 2017 following the introduction of new taxi laws.

The process of obtaining a taxi driver's license in Denmark is not an easy one, and requires extensive knowledge of the routes in the city. If you have your destination written down your taxi driver should have no problem finding it. One thing that you will notice is that many of the taxi drivers are immigrants, and therefore while they may speak passable Danish there is no guarantee that they will speak English.

CYCLING

Just over a quarter of Danes use their bicycles for transportation on a daily basis. Bike lanes exist in most major cities, and in the countryside there are special bike paths running between the major towns. Cycling is a good way to get to know the country and to meet people. It is very environmentally friendly, healthy, and fully in keeping with the principles of *Jante*. You will therefore find people a little more approachable from the saddle of a bicycle.

Helmets are advisable, though not compulsory. Danish cyclists are unfortunately no better than their motorized counterparts in automobiles when it comes to road etiquette. They are generally intolerant of mistakes until they find out that you are a foreigner and then, after apologizing for abusing you, they will usually gently inform you of the nature of your mistake.

One thing you may want to keep in mind is that it is customary to use your bell to warn cyclists in front and behind when you are about to pass. It is also obligatory for you to stop for alighting bus passengers at bus stops. Lights must be used, front and back, during the hours of darkness, and the police are quite vigilant about this; the fine for noncompliance is around 750 kroner. Bicycle theft is rife in Denmark, so remember to lock your bike whenever you leave it. Bikes are allowed on trains and ferries at an extra charge. Taxis will also take a bike for an extra charge. Bikes can be rented easily throughout Denmark, although helmets are not usually included in the rental fee.

FLYING

Distances in Denmark are rather short by American standards. Domestic flights usually take little more than forty-five minutes from takeoff to landing. The majority of Denmark's domestic flights are operated by SAS. SAS also operates routes between Copenhagen, Århus, and Ålborg. There are usually a number of opportunities for getting discounts on internal flights, and it is sometimes worth checking any special offers as air travel in Denmark is expensive. Service on Danish flights is efficient and polite, without being too friendly.

HEALTH

As in most of Western Europe, there are no special immunizations required for traveling to Denmark. If, however, you are coming from a country that is classified as an infected area with a particular disease, then you may be required to prove that you have been immunized against that disease. This proof is usually required to be in the form of an International Health Certificate showing the inoculations received.

Visitors from outside the EU should ensure that they have medical insurance to cover the costs of minor illnesses or ailments while in Denmark. Should you be unfortunate enough to be involved in an accident while in Denmark, medical services are provided free of charge. This is also the case if you suffer a relapse of a chronic, preexisting condition and are too ill to return to your home country.

In general, medical personnel in Denmark, while efficient, lack the bedside manner that you may be used to at home. Doctors in Denmark treat the illness, not the patient. Danes are frank and open in describing their medical conditions, no matter how intimate, and a Danish doctor will find the usual Anglo-Saxon reticence in this regard somewhat perplexing. Almost all doctors in Denmark speak English with a reasonable degree of fluency. There may be some language difficulties in relation to particular medical conditions and diseases, or the description of certain symptoms. If it is likely that you will need to consult a doctor during your stay, you may think it worth buying a bilingual dictionary.

Should you become ill outside normal surgery hours then there is a twenty-four-hour service known as *Lægevagten* available in the larger cities. A similar dental service is also available. The telephone numbers for both services can be found at the front of any local telephone directory.

In Denmark controlled drugs are available only with a prescription, *recept,* from a Scandinavian medical practitioner. Many of these drugs may be available without prescription in other countries, including the USA. If you are taking regular medication in your home country, it is a good idea to check whether a prescription would be required for this medication in Denmark should the need arise. Pharmacies, *Apotek,* are open from 10:00 a.m. until 6:00 p.m. on weekdays and from 10:00 a.m. to 2:00 p.m. on Saturdays. For service outside these hours you will be able to find a twenty-four-hour pharmacy, *Døgnapotek,* in the larger cities.

Tap water is perfectly safe to drink in Denmark, and the standard of hygiene in bars, cafés, and restaurants is high. All businesses serving food to the general public are regularly inspected and required by law to display health certificates. These certificates are in Danish but also use a "smiley face" grading system: the more smiley faces, the better the standard of hygiene.

AIDS and HIV infection are not widespread in Denmark. There is, however, a worrying trend upward in the figures of those infected. Medical authorities put this down to more relaxed attitudes toward the risk of infection and the fall in the number of people using protection. This is mainly in the heterosexual population.

Denmark is a very wheelchair-friendly country, and people will go out of their way to help those with physical difficulties. Do not be shy in asking for assistance should you need it, particularly on public transportation, as all buses and trains are equipped with foldaway ramps, which the driver will take out on request.

SAFETY

In general, Denmark is a very safe country for visitors—one of the safest in Europe. You should always, however, take the usual precautions with regard to personal safety and the safety of your belongings. While there are no real "no go" areas in Denmark, in Copenhagen the Nørrebro area does occasionally suffer from incidents involving local gangs and drug-related crime; however the number is extremely small by American standards. Serious crime is rare, with the most common crimes probably being petty theft and shoplifting. Denmark is occasionally visited by some more delinquent tourists determined to relieve their fellow travelers of the weight of their cash. When these pickpockets hit, they usually do so for a short time in the summer. Be sensible about keeping your cash and credit cards secure and out of sight.

Should you become a victim of this, or any other type of crime, report it to the police immediately. You will find them both helpful and informative. There is actually a good chance that your wallet or purse will eventually be found, as most of these thieves simply take the cash and dump the rest in the nearest garbage can.

Women traveling alone should have no problems in Denmark, culturally speaking. Denmark is very much a progressive country, and a woman traveling alone is not seen as unusual. One should, however, take sensible precautions about one's safety, as one would at home.

chapter eight

BUSINESS
BRIEFING

THE ECONOMY

The Danish economy is one of the strongest in
Europe, having a balanced state budget, a stable
currency pegged to the euro, low inflation, and
low interest rates. Denmark has one of the world's
lowest levels of income inequality and one of the
highest standards of living according to World
Bank figures. It is a small, open economy, geared
to trade with other countries. Denmark's most
important trading partner is Germany, followed
by Sweden, Britain, and the USA. Norway

and Japan are also significant trading partners. Denmark is a member state of the EU as well as the WTO and the OECD. Industrial products account for over 70 percent of its total exports. This is a radical reversal of the situation before the Second World War, when the Danish economy was based primarily on agriculture. Indeed, Denmark is the third-largest oil producer in Western Europe, after Norway and Britain.

Denmark has sought to regulate economic activity, as well as inflation, through fiscal policy, while monetary policy has been more and more aimed at ensuring a stable exchange rate for the Danish krone.

THE DANISH WORK ETHIC

When the Danes are at work they are there to work, and they are very focused on their job. They do not see the workplace as a social environment. The Danish work ethic is very strong, and Danes are hard workers. They also feel that they should have a say in how things are run in the workplace, no matter what their position, and their employers respect this. While salary is important, most Danes would consider that the first priority of their job is that it should be interesting and challenging.

Danes are ambitious and like to succeed, but are not overly interested in the outward show of success. For them success is much more a matter of personal and professional satisfaction which does not necessarily require the validation of an executive suite or the key to the executive washroom. However, younger Danes are becoming more interested in the trappings of success, and the Jante law seems to be losing its grip on the younger generation.

OFFICE SENSE AND SENSIBILITY

One of the chief characteristics of the Danish office environment is the openness and lack of formality between employers and employees. Teamwork is central to the Danish way of doing things, and there is no place that this is more apparent than in the office. Manners between colleagues are also generally informal and relaxed. Danish parents give priority to their family life and aim to be home at the end of the afternoon. Most business meetings are scheduled to end between 4:00 and 5:00 p.m. to allow for this.

If there is any social life in the office, then it normally happens during the coffee and lunch breaks. Long business lunches are highly unusual, unless with visitors from client or parent companies. Some offices will have a get-together for a beer at the end of the working week.

All businesses in Denmark respect the tradition of the Christmas office lunch, or *julefrokost*. This is the social climax of the year for all workplaces. Some may also have a party or social event in the summer.

Social Equality

The Danish workplace is less hierarchically
structured than that of, for example, America.
Generally the chain of command between bosses
and their employees is short. In principle everyone,
regardless of salary, position, or duties, is regarded
as equal. Danish bosses tend to listen more to their
staff than those in other countries, and regard them
as experts in their own fields. In many companies
the bosses are regarded more as team leaders than
decision makers. During meetings as well as in the
decision-making process everyone is encouraged to
voice an opinion. The final decision, however, still
lies in the hands of the boss.

Social interaction takes place between all
levels, and giving preferential treatment to anyone
is actively discouraged. The idea of equality is
entrenched in the Danish psyche. Competence is
deemed more important than one's position in the

workplace or station in life. Danish workers regard their own personal responsibility and contribution very highly—much more than their salary or job security.

Education and Training

Most people in the Danish corporate world are highly educated, as promotion is largely dependent on excellent academic results combined with performance and experience. Most Danes who go to university leave with a master's degree, unless they drop out; courses of studies at Danish universities do not end at the bachelor's level.

A feature of the Danish office environment is the emphasis put on further training. Nine out of ten companies offer further training to their employees within their first year of employment. This may take the form of external courses, of courses and training seminars at the workplace, or of longer courses and programs, such as an MBA. Denmark is among those European countries that feature the highest company investment in further training for their employees compared to wage costs, and lies third on the international list, compiled by the International Institute for Management Development, of those countries that prioritize further training most highly.

Informality

People speak openly about their private lives with their colleagues. They talk about their families, problems, vacations, and what they do in their spare time. The Danes have a reputation for being informal, and this can also be seen in the office environment. The office dress code is generally relatively relaxed for both men and women. Although many Danish men may still wear a suit this is often a matter of personal choice rather than adherence to any formal dress code. There are, however, some companies that still have a dress code and therefore it is worth checking this while planning your trip. If they are meeting a person that they already know, Danes are likely to be less formally dressed than they might be if it were an initial meeting.

At first business meetings Danes will generally introduce themselves using their first name and surname, accompanied by a handshake. The exchange of business cards usually takes place at the end of a meeting. Danes rarely bring gifts to business meetings, and do not expect them in return. If, however, you feel that things are going well, or if you are meeting a Dane you have already established an acquaintance with, then feel free to bring a small gift. A paperweight or some other office item with a company logo would be appropriate.

Language
Many of the larger Danish companies have adopted English as their corporate language. In most companies, the general principle

governing internal day-to-day communication is that each specific situation determines whether the Danish or English language should be used. Most companies place a great deal of weight on communicating in English when there are foreigners present in all situations, from meetings through presentations and internal messages to informal chat between colleagues. Unpretentiousness is central to any social interaction in the Danish workplace. People will tend to underplay their role and qualifications, and you will hardly ever hear anyone promote themselves or their own skills.

Danes are very direct when commenting on work. This should not be taken as a personal attack, as it is not meant as such. Criticism is regarded as something that has to do with one's work, not oneself. You will find that Danes in general are always ready to voice their opinions on many matters, work-related or otherwise. Unlike their Swedish cousins, Danes are not afraid of confrontation. They will, however, try to avoid a disagreement becoming too personal. Danes always prefer to discuss differences rather than argue over them, if possible.

TIME KEEPING

A point that must be stressed again, especially in relation to the business world, is punctuality. The Danes are almost religious in their sense of punctuality and expect others to be on time. This is especially true in the case of business meetings. If you are going to be delayed for any amount of time, then call ahead. While Danes would never openly criticize tardiness on your behalf, this would not leave them with a good impression. Ideally, arrive neither early nor late. Danes take pride in having as full an appointment schedule as possible, and it therefore doesn't take a lot to mess it up!

TAKING A BREAK

There are two breaks in the Danish working day: the morning coffee break and the lunch break, taken at around 10:00 a.m. and 12:00 noon respectively. Danes use these opportunities to socialize at work and chat with their colleagues. The subjects for discussion can range from politics to marital problems to the price of pork at the local supermarket.

Telling All

I remember once taking a coffee break with a female student while teaching her English. We had barely sat down when she began to tell me about the rather difficult divorce she was going through. Being new to the country, I was somewhat taken aback, until it was later explained to me that this was just another example of Danish openness and a perfectly natural topic of conversation for a Dane.

Many Danes bring a *madpakke,* or packed lunch, to work, which they eat while sitting at their desks or in the office lunchroom. In larger offices and businesses, cafeteria food is supplied at a reduced cost, subsidized by the employer. As the usual lunch break only lasts half an hour, going out to lunch is neither practical nor popular. Traditionally it was acceptable to have a beer during the morning and lunch breaks. This tradition has largely died out, but is still in evidence among some blue-collar workers.

WOMEN IN BUSINESS

Denmark has one of the highest levels of female participation in the workplace in the world. Roughly 74 percent of Danish women are active in the labor market, compared to 79 percent of men. Despite this, women are not yet equally represented on the upper levels of the corporate ladder. This situation is still the subject of much

debate in Denmark. In general women have shown
themselves to be at least as good as their male
colleagues in management, and in many cases
better. The Gender Equality Board is the watchdog
body in cases of sex discrimination in Denmark.

Female participation in the workplace has been
greatly assisted by the child-care provisions of the
Danish social welfare model, which have given
women in Denmark the freedom to develop their
careers. It is perhaps interesting to note that, despite
the progressive attitudes of the Danes, women still
appear to bear the primary responsibility for bringing
up children. Women visiting Denmark from more
conservative societies may find that it is easier to
initiate meetings and social engagements with men.

TRADE UNIONS

Danish commercial life is still dominated by the
remnants of the old guild system. Almost every job
requires some form of occupational training, and

that training is usually thorough no matter what the occupation is.

Unemployment benefits in Denmark are administered by the unions. The Danish government allocates a sum to each union that the union itself then administers. While you do not have to be a member of a union to be entitled to benefit, you will have to apply to a union-administered *A-Kasse* to receive it.

Over 70 percent of Danish wage earners are members of a union. Union membership is particularly high among skilled and unskilled workers, although membership is also common among wage earners with a higher education. University degree holders have more flexibility in their choice of whether or not to join a union. This is primarily due to the fact that they negotiate their salary and work conditions on an individual basis, especially in the private sector.

Smaller unions are unified in larger, nationwide associations. For degree holders the most important unions are the Society of Danish Engineers, the Association of Business and Administration, the Danish Association of Masters and Ph.D.s, and the Association of Danish Lawyers and Economists.

Employers also have their own organizations, the largest of these being the Danish Employers' Confederation, the Confederation of Danish Industries, the Danish Commerce and Services, and the Federation of Employers for Trade, Transport, and Services.

Unions and employers' organizations also negotiate with the government under a scheme known as tripartite cooperation. The negotiations usually concern issues surrounding labor market policy on matters such as unemployment and insurance issues.

SETTLING DIFFERENCES

Like most interactions in Danish life, negotiations between unions and management are largely conducted on the basis of consensus, if at all possible. It is rare that the two sides are unable to come to an agreement.

In Denmark, unlike many other European countries, the regulation of the labor market is by agreement rather than by law. Unions and employers negotiate agreements collectively in most cases while, as stated above, employees with a high level of education will normally negotiate their salaries on an individual basis. These agreements by and large replace legislation in the area of wages and labor conditions.

Nearly 80 percent of the Danish labor market is subject to these broad collective agreements, which contribute to its peace and stability. They have also led to a high degree of flexibility in the labor market and, as a consequence, to high mobility. From a total workforce of 2.875 million, 800,000 positions are occupied every year. This figure is a combination of changes from one job to another as well as new positions created in the labor market. It still indicates, however, the high degree of mobility in the workforce. The Danish labor market, therefore, bears a closer resemblance to the US model than to that of other European countries. The Danish social welfare system is intended to provide a safety net for those who might suffer as a result of this flexibility in the labor market.

PRESENTATION STYLE

The Danes in general speak directly, and this comes across in their presentation style. They will want to get down to business with as little fuss as possible, and will always be well-prepared and armed with a great many facts to back up their arguments. Danes never interrupt, nor do they expect to be interrupted. When giving a presentation they expect to be listened to patiently until the end, when there will be time for questions and answers.

Danes are very hard workers, and try to use every minute at work as effectively as possible. As a result their presentation style is swift, concise, and with as little elaboration as possible, though they pay attention to detail, and will use printed papers, graphs, and charts copiously to clarify points. Body language is confined to small gestures.

Always remember that the Dane giving the presentation in English is using his or her second language. Be prepared to seek clarification of any points that may seem unclear to you by taking notes and raising them after the presentation is finished. Danes express their opinions freely and you may find them blunt in their style of presentation. This lack of diplomacy can sometimes be a shock at first, but it is simply the Danish way of communicating.

NEGOTIATING

First and foremost, yet again, be punctual. The importance of this cannot be overstressed when dealing with Danes. If you are taking a taxi to your meeting, order it to pick you up in plenty of time so you can be certain of arriving on time. Business cards are desirable, but don't have them translated into Danish on the reverse. Most Danes understand English, and to do so would merely display your lack of knowledge of their country and people. If you are representing a company that was founded more than, say, ten years ago, it would be a good idea to indicate this on your business card. Danes, like most Scandinavians, appreciate stability in the firms they deal with.

When you arrive at your destination, your Danish hosts will introduce themselves with a handshake, and you should follow suit. If there are women present you may feel free to initiate a handshake with them also. Always shake hands from a standing position, never sitting down, and make eye contact while doing so. After the initial introductions the Danes will quickly shift to addressing you and everyone else by first names. Shake hands again when leaving.

Meetings will be held according to a set agenda, and the pace is usually quick. The meeting may begin with a few minutes of small talk, but you will probably get straight down to business. This will depend on the person leading the meeting. Should there be small talk, the easiest thing is to let the Danes set the topic of conversation, which will usually be your home country.

As with presentations, the Danish negotiating style is direct and to the point. Be receptive to their input and respond in positive tones; remember if they criticize it is the work they are criticizing and not you personally. Subjective feelings play no role, so stick to objective facts. Your counterparts will almost always follow universal Danish behavioral norms rather than react personally to a particular situation.

Do not give preferential treatment to, for example, the person leading the negotiations from the Danish side. The idea of equality is entrenched in Danish society.

Bear in mind that the Danes are very environmentally aware, and the introduction of any plans that would have an adverse effect on the environment will not be well received.

Remember, too, that for your Danish counterparts the meeting is being held in a foreign language. We often overestimate the fluency of non-native English speakers because their language skills are better than ours. They may not understand everything you say. Try to speak in a fairly measured way, without being so slow as to be blatantly obvious, and avoid raising your voice. (Native English speakers might try to adopt a pace similar to that of the late British Prime Minister Margaret Thatcher.)

Avoid the use of idiomatic expressions, as your counterparts may not understand them or may misinterpret them. Express yourself as simply as possible. Break down what you want to say into manageable chunks of information. As a rule, limit your thoughts to one idea per sentence—this will help to make your comments clear and understandable.

During a negotiation Danes will not see establishing a rapport as being a part of the procedure. They will stick to the subject at hand. Once an agreement has been reached and contracts signed you can be sure that things will move forward. Above all, Danes are, in general, a people of their word.

Small Talk

One Danish businessman remarked that if you want to have small talk at a meeting you should add an extra ten minutes to the agenda! When things do turn to small talk, avoid asking personal questions about private life, religion, income, or family. The Danes consider it inappropriate and rude to try to get personal with someone whom you have only just met. Also, complimenting someone on their appearance could be seen as frivolous and might cause offense.

Danes have a history of tolerance, so avoid criticizing other people or systems. You will find the Danish sense of humor a little drier and more reserved than, for example, the American. Remember that humor is very culture specific, so be careful when using it.

DECISION MAKING

As we have seen, while the Danish workplace does have a hierarchical structure, it is less rigid than that of many other countries. In general Danes are group-oriented; subjects are discussed and a consensus is reached. Decisions based on a vote are uncommon—to vote would highlight a division. Discussion allows people to see a problem from numerous points of view. The final decision, however, is made by a leader, which makes the decision-making process less laborious than, say, with many Swedish companies, in which decisions are made by consensus alone.

Bargaining in the American sense—start high and go low—is not a part of the Danish negotiating technique. The Danes will try to formulate a sensible, realistic first offer that they feel should satisfy all parties concerned. Treating this first offer as an opening bid would be a mistake. They will be at best confused and at worst offended by your seeming rejection of what they see as a sensible resolution of matters.

Playing "hardball" with Danes is a tricky business, to say the least. The aim of negotiations Danish style is to achieve a win/win situation. If you play hardball they may perceive you as obstructionist and uncooperative. At the very least it will create an *uhyggelig*, or uncomfortable, atmosphere, and given the importance of *hygge* to the Danes this is something you will want to avoid.

On the completion of a successful negotiation you may wish to give a gift to your counterpart. Should you receive a gift in return you may open it right away, in front of the giver, rather than waiting. Danes like alcohol, so wine, whiskey, or similar items make good gifts. Good-quality chocolates or desk items are also considered appropriate gifts.

CONTRACTS

The Danish legal system is based on "Roman" law. That is to say, only the legislature can make law. America, the British Isles, and most English-speaking countries employ the system of law known as "common law." Under common law the courts can make new law, and precedent, or old decisions, can be very important. The fact that Denmark works under a Roman system has implications for contracts drawn up under Danish law.

The first thing you will notice is that a Danish contract is shorter and simpler than its common-law counterpart. This is because a lot of the matters that in a common-law jurisdiction would have to be covered in the contract are already covered by Danish law, and there is therefore no need to include them in the contract. Conversely, a Dane will find a common-law contract very long and wordy, and it is worth taking the time to go through it in detail. This will ensure that there is no confusion and will be appreciated by your Danish counterpart. For your own part, an awareness of the Danish law is essential if you are to know what a contract made under Danish law covers, and therefore hiring a Danish lawyer, or *advokat*, is well worth the extra expense.

Because of the simplicity of contracts under Danish law Danes tend not to have teams of lawyers sitting in on negotiations at the initial phase. They would see it as unnecessary and wasteful. Due to the sheer amount of business being done between Denmark and common-law jurisdictions, however, the more detailed, common-law type of contract is starting to take hold in Denmark.

Danes are highly honorable. If they give you their word on something they will stick to it, and will expect the same of you. Once a contract is signed, the Danes will expect it to be honored to the letter.

CORPORATE ENTERTAINMENT?

Put simply, the Danes in general are not good at corporate entertainment. It is not part of their business culture. They themselves rarely go out for a lunch break. As well as this, most like to go home to their families after close of business. The usual form of corporate entertainment in Denmark is the business lunch, between 12:00 noon and 2:00 p.m. In the cities this will usually be held in one of the many popular cellar cafés. Lunch here usually consists of large, open-faced sandwiches, which should be eaten with the knife and fork provided.

If you are invited to dinner, it is likely to be at your host's home, and if your spouse is traveling with you then it is more than likely that he or she will be included in the invitation. You may like to take a gift. (See page 87.)

WORKING WITH DANES

Danes tend to be literal in their interpretation of what you say. If you say you will be back in five minutes then they will expect you to be back in five minutes! One should therefore be very careful when giving an estimate, for example, of how long it may take to complete a contract; they will take you at your word, literally. If a Dane gives their word on something then they will usually honor it and will expect the same of you.

Should you employ Danes, you should remember that they will expect to make more of a contribution than you may be used to. They will be free with their opinions and criticisms, and surprised if you take them personally.

chapter nine

COMMUNICATING

Language should be no bar to a visit to Denmark as most Danish people speak reasonably fluent English. This is because English has been a compulsory subject in Danish schools for decades. While you will find that most of the Danes you meet are quite capable of conversing in English, the level will depend largely on their age and standard of education. Danes speaking English can sound a little abrupt at times. You should bear in mind that this is more than likely a linguistic failing rather than intentional.

DANISH

Danish is the official language of Denmark, Greenland, and the Faroe Islands. It is a member of the Indo-European family, and is part of the North Germanic group, together with Icelandic, Faroese, Norwegian, and Swedish. Over history Danish has adopted words from many other languages, notably German, French, and, in the twentieth century especially, English. Danish is written in the Roman alphabet with the addition of three letters: æ, ø, and å (pronounced, respectively, as in the words "ale," "turn," and "oh"). Those whose native language is English generally find learning Danish easier than most.

In creating new words, Danish tends to use or adapt existing words, and consequently the largest Danish dictionaries contain no more than 200,000 words. This is done by compounding words together to form a new word such as *langtidsplanlægge*, which is composed of three words, *lang, tid, planlægge*, and means "to plan long-term."

DANISH ENGLISH

Although they speak English well, most Danes do not make any distinction between American and British English. Owing to the influence of American films you will find that the majority of Danes speak American English. Unfortunately some Danish people are not familiar with the type of language acceptable in polite English conversation. As a result they may, on rare occasions, use inappropriate language. This is purely the result of lack of knowledge and is not intended to be offensive. Any non-native speakers of English will make some mistakes and have some difficulties.

Typically Danes have difficulty with the English "r" sound. This is mainly due to the fact that the Danish "*r*" sound is fetched from deep down in the tonsils and is very guttural in nature. Their use of prepositions will sometimes be incorrect but not usually so as to confuse meaning. They will also have problems with verbs, which in Danish are not conjugated in the present tense. A Dane might therefore say something like "You is feeling okay now?" "Is" and "are" are very commonly confused.

Danes also tend to run into trouble in the use of prepositions, often translating directly from Danish. Thus they may say "be good to" rather than "be good at," "north for" rather than "north of," "to work on an office" rather than "to work at an office," "written on English" rather than "written in English," "look on" rather than "look at," "look after" rather than "look for," and "look of" rather than "look after."

LET'S TALK ABOUT IT

One thing that you will soon notice about Danes is their love of discussion and debate. There is nothing they like more than to sit outside a café and discuss all manner of subjects. Most Danes are prepared to talk about anything, and have an opinion on everything.

You will, in general, find it very difficult to dissuade a Dane from an opinion that he or she has already formed. Unless, that is, you can provide some facts to show that they are in error. You may also find Danes to be rather frank in their way of expressing themselves—it is their way. Should you disagree with an opinion a Dane will expect you to speak up—remember this is discussing, not arguing, therefore no feelings are hurt. In general when discussing, Danes address the issue, not the person. Consequently if you ask a Dane for his or her opinion, then that is precisely what you will get, in all its unvarnished glory. The Danish attitude is that if you don't want to hear their opinion then you shouldn't ask for it. Danish men, for instance, have no problems with the vexing "Do I look fat in this?" question from a spouse!

CUT THE COMMERCIAL

Direct and honest in their speech, the Danes tend neither to understate nor to overstate. Their communication style is blunt and undiplomatic, and may be misinterpreted as being rude. They will usually back up what they say with relevant facts and will expect the same of you. Danes are very reluctant to give an opinion on anything without being able to support it with facts. Superficiality is not a Danish trait and you should try to avoid it when talking to them.

You may notice a subtle regional variation in style. People from rural areas, especially Jutland, tend to speak at a slower pace and be a little more reserved in their opinions than city dwellers. They are also a little harder to get to know initially.

When talking to Danes it is best not to be too inquisitive at first. Let them dictate the pace of the conversation for a while, and you will soon get a feel for things. They will be very interested in where you come from and will want to know as much about your country as you do about them.

In conversation Danes are comfortable with silences and do not feel the need to rush in and fill the gap. Above all avoid doing so unless what you have to say is relevant.

Another habit you may come across, especially on first meeting Danish people in a group situation, is that they will begin speaking to you in English and then, after a polite interval, resume conversation with someone else in Danish. You have to remember that speaking for a prolonged period in English is quite difficult for a Dane and can be quite a strain. This no reflection on you and should not be taken as such.

BODY LANGUAGE

Danes are rather restrained in their body language, which, as far as expressiveness goes, lies somewhere in between the British and the Swedes. They have a tendency to concentrate on the spoken word and regard elaborate body language as a hindrance to good communication. They will, however, use a great deal of eye contact when speaking to you. This may, at first, seem intimidating, but they are simply indicating that they are listening and interested in what you have to say. There are no particular pitfalls for the Anglo-Saxon visitor in Danish body language. Most of the hand gestures that are used in, for example, Britain or America, carry the same meaning in Denmark. This is largely due to the influence of American films.

THE MEDIA
The Danish state-owned and -run station, DR, has two television stations, DR1 and DR2. There are also numerous commercial television stations such as TV2, TV2 Zulu, TV Charlie, TV3, TV3+, and TV4, to name but a few. These stations are supplemented by the usual cable stations, such as MTV, BBC World, and Prime, CNN. English-made programs are broadcast with subtitles in Danish. The Danish do not dub television programs or movies, relying on subtitles instead. The only exceptions to this rule are films and cartoons made for young children.

Most apartment buildings have cable TV, and the monthly fee is included in the rent. Danish television is rather more liberal than its Anglo-Saxon counterparts. There are also various radio stations on offer and DR1 broadcasts an English news bulletin at 8:00 a.m. every day.

You may notice that the Danish interviewing style is less confrontational than that of, say, the USA or England. Danish interviewers strive to sound objective, and always try to ensure that the interviewee gets a chance to respond to their questions as fully as possible. Many Danes were shocked recently when their Minister for Foreign Affairs was "grilled" on British television over Denmark's strict immigration laws. They felt that the interviewer was far too personal and didn't give the minister a chance to give a proper response to his questions.

Newspapers and Magazines

There are more than forty-eight newspapers in Denmark at the time of writing. Of these *MX Metro Express* has the highest circulation, followed by *Politiken*. Free newspapers, lifestyle magazines, and specialist newspapers abound. One reason for this is that Danes like to be well-informed about what is going on in the world around them. They expect a newspaper to give the facts of a story followed, if necessary, by a well-informed debate. The more sensationalist side of newspaper journalism is represented by the two popular tabloid newspapers *BT* and *Ekstra Bladet*.

There are many English-language newspapers available in the large Danish cities. Among these are the *New York Times International Edition*, *USA Today*, the *Wall Street Journal*, the *Financial Times*, the *Times*, and the *Guardian*. The news magazines *Time*, the *Economist*, and *Newsweek* are also widely available. The best place to look for these is in a railway station newsstand.

TECHNOLOGY AND SERVICES

The Danes love new technology and services. Very few private homes in Denmark are without broadband Internet. Smartphones are now an accepted part of life. If you should have to cancel an appointment, or are running late and wish to let a Dane know, you can send a message; however, the personal touch of a voice call is still recommended.

You will find that the vast majority of communications, especially in business, are conducted by e-mail. Danes like the speed and convenience of this form of communication, and are not afraid of using it to communicate with English speakers either.

Telephone

The country code for Denmark is +45, and there are no local codes, so you simply dial 45 followed by the eight-digit number of the person you are calling. Similarly, cell phones do not have a special area code.

Owing to the growth of the cell phone market in Denmark, public pay phones have fallen out of use and there are fewer and fewer of them to be found on the streets. Should you be bringing your cell phone with you, check that it is compatible with the European GSM system. On answering the telephone a Dane will say, for example, "*Det er Jon,*" meaning "It's Jon." This is the standard way of answering the telephone in Denmark.

USEFUL NUMBERS	
Emergency Services	112
Directory Services for Denmark	118
International Directory Services	113
All telephone operators speak English.	

Mail

The Danish postal service prides itself on being the most efficient in Europe. Letters posted in Denmark for delivery within its borders usually arrive the next day. The post offices, or *posthus*, also have banking facilities and a ticket-ordering service for concerts, theaters, and so on. Post offices are open from 10:00 a.m. to 6:00 p.m. on weekdays and from 10:00 a.m. to 1:00 p.m. on Saturdays. All mailboxes are colored red.

CONCLUSION

Denmark is a beautiful country, on a human scale. It may lack the majestic scenery of Sweden and its cities may not possess the grandeur of Paris or Rome, but it is an intimate country that embraces rather than overwhelms. Like its people, the country takes a little time to understand and appreciate. From the astronomer Tycho Brahe to Maersk Shipping, the Danish people have made important contributions to the world in the realms of culture, science, commerce, and politics. They are still contributing today, whether it be through development in the Third World or through the Copenhagen Agreement, which saw the accession to the EU of many former members of the Soviet Bloc. Denmark has a voice in world affairs. It may not be a big voice, but it is listened to.

The effort you put into getting to know Denmark and its people will be amply rewarded. You will discover that the Danes are far from the

cold, reserved Scandinavians that many typically
think they are. You will find their honesty and
openness refreshing, and will not mistakenly
take offense where none is meant. You may
even benefit from seeing the familiar through
a different set of eyes. In this book we hope to
have provided a first step on a journey not just to
another country, but to another culture, another,
more positive, way of looking at the world.

Further Reading

Anderson, Barbara Gallatin. *First Fieldwork: The Misadventures of an Anthropologist.* Illinois: Waveland Press, 1989.

Bonetto, Cristian. *Lonely Planet Pocket Copenhagen.* Dublin: Lonely Planet Global Limited, 2018.

Høeg, Peter, and Barbera Haveland (translator). *Tales of the Night.* London: The Harvill Press, 1997.

Jacobsen, Helge Seidelin. *An Outline History of Denmark.* Copenhagen: Høst & Sons Forlag, 1986.

Jespersen, Knud. J. V. *A History of Denmark.* London: Palgrave Macmillan, 2004.

Lampe, David. *Hitler's Savage Canary: A History of Danish Resistance In World War Two.* Barnsley: Frontline Books, 2010.

Ronberg, Gert (ed.). *Eyewitness Travel Phrase Book: Danish.* New York: Dorling Kindersley Publishing, 1999.

Russell, Helen. *The Year of Living Danishly: Uncovering the Secrets of the World's Happiest Country.* London: Icon Books, 2015.

Sommar, Ingrid. *Scandinavian Style.* London: Carlton Books, 2003.

Wiking, Meik. *The Little Book of Hygge: The Danish Way to Live Well.* London: Penguin Life, 2016.

Index